EVE~
SCOTT THOMPSON AND
HIS "CROWNING ACHIEVEMENT"*
BUDDY COLE

"Thompson has been making liberal North Americans
uncomfortable about their attitudes towards homosexuality
for over a decade now, and he has no intention of stopping
anytime soon! He is best known for his character 'Buddy,'
a flaming gay nightclub owner who delivered monologues
that bordered on the theatrical and represent some of the
most radically original television work seen on
American TV, ever."
—*Wyoming Eagle*

"Buddy Cole [is] the kind of unapologetic bon vivant who
uses the term 'fag' with pride."
—*Artvoice*

"[Thompson's] crowning achievement is Buddy Cole . . .
who owns a bar and pontificates brilliantly on all manner
of TV-taboo subjects."
—*Bay Area Reporter**

Buddy Babylon

The Autobiography of Buddy Cole

Scott Thompson
and Paul Bellini

A Dell Trade Paperback

A DELL TRADE PAPERBACK

Published by
Dell Publishing
a division of
Bantam Doubleday Dell Publishing Group, Inc.
1540 Broadway
New York, New York 10036

Book design by Susan Maksuta

Thompson, Scott, 1959–
    Buddy Babylon: the autobiography of Buddy Cole / Scott Thompson and Paul Bellini.
        p.   cm.
    ISBN 0-440-50828-2
    I. Bellini, Paul.   II. Title.
PR9199.3.T4725B83   1998
791.45′028′092—dc21
[B]   97-46877
                                                                           CIP

Printed in the United States of America

Published simultaneously in Canada

June 1998

10 9 8 7 6 5 4 3 2

BVG

to
My Three Amuses
Paul Agnew, Brian Hill, and Allan Kerr
from whom I stole so much.

May this dedication be enough flattery
to avoid a costly lawsuit.

Buddy Cole,
March 1998, Toronto

"There's nothing too good for a man, if he's a good man."
—Tennessee Williams, *The Rose Tattoo*

"I may have been born yesterday, but I still went shopping."
—Carol Beauchamp

Contents

Buddy
Babylon

By way of an introduction . . .

They say that the exact circumstances of a person's birth determine the course of the rest of his or her life. In my case, this was profoundly so. Let me explain. I was born on February 29, 1960, a leap year, thereby celebrating my birthday every four years. It was inevitable I would be a homosexual. Imagine. Even when I'm eighty, in some places I'll still be too young to drink.

To look at me, you'd think that I was hatched from a Fabergé egg, the scion of a lost branch of one of the Royal Houses of Europe. For years, this is what I actually told people. But now that I've been given money to tell my life story, I feel the truth threatening to break through. No, dear reader, I was not born with a silver spoon in my mouth. More like a rusty fork. Now, before I launch you on the thrill ride that is my life, I must give you some background information. Think of it as foreplay. So lay back and spread your legs because some of this stuff is pretty hard to swallow. You'll need every hole you've got.

I was born on a pig farm in northern Quebec, Canada, in a little hamlet of two thousand people called St. Hubert sur la Lac, or St. Hubert on the Lake. As far as I know, there was never actually a Saint Hubert, but there was a St. Hubert's

Chicken restaurant nearby, so that must have been where the name came from. I was the last of twenty-three children. I was christened Charles Butterick Cole, the Charles was after Charles Boyer, Maman's favourite actor, the Butterick after my paternal grandfather. Everyone called me Butterick though until one day my father shortened it to Buddy by mistake and it stuck. My parents, Angus Sean Cole, a lusty Scotsman who arrived in Quebec in 1920 at the age of fifteen, and my mother, Giselle Christianne Lavigne, the only child of Quebecois pig farmers, met at a cockfight in 1930 and married soon after. My family operated in both official languages. We spoke French to our mother, and Scottish to our father. From what I saw, they loved each other very much. That's probably why I turned out so stable. Maman doted on Papa's brusque Scottish virility, and Papa adored Maman, who was no looker. But she had a *jolie* spirit, a good heart, and most importantly, came with a farm. People today are almost offended that my parents had such a big family, that they were somehow enviro-terrorists, but I figure if it took that many children to produce me, then it was worth the extra burden on the planet.

Our farm was at the end of a long gravel road about a mile from town, on the edge of a beautiful body of water called Lac d'Eau, or Water Lake. Directly opposite the shore was a tiny island about five hundred yards away. It was called L'Isle des Memoires, or Island of Memories. According to Indian legend, some Indian princess, Canada's Pocahontas, hit her head on a branch on the island and lost her memory, and we're supposed to remember her or something. I was always vague on the details, but it was a powerful ceremony held each year when the Indians drove up in their Jeeps with cases of beer for the occasion. Most of the population worked in the nearby copper mine. Many of my brothers ended up working there, but luckily I escaped that fate or this would have been a very different book. Although we were not impoverished, there were so many mouths to feed that for all intents and purposes

I grew up poor. Luckily, I was not brought up religious. I think that was because my mother was Catholic and my father was Presbyterian, so rather than fight about it, it was just easier for us to be nothing. Let's face it, dear reader, my parents were too pooped for the Pope.

As I look back over the finished manuscript, I remember so many other stories that I should have told, and so many lovers who will hate me for not being mentioned (you know who you are, Henry), but this is what came out—a series of true events arranged in such a way as to entertain, inform, illuminate, and above all, make me look good. Who knows, if this thing is big, and I don't see how it can't be, maybe there will be a sequel. I know one thing, though: it had better be a much bigger advance. I practically starved on the miserable stipend my editor gave me this time. I know it's petty, but I can't help but gloat that Whoopi Goldberg's book, *Book*, bombed. She should have called it *Whoopi Babylon*. But this is not the time for bitterness. That's for the story.

Some of my tales are not for the fainthearted. They may contain adult situations and language that may not be appropriate for younger readers. In other words, it's rated NC-17, so if you are under the age of seventeen and are reading this book, you're busted. All I ask is that you don't just race ahead to the dirty parts, like I did with *The Godfather*.

You will notice throughout the text that I seemingly reproduce conversations perfectly that no normal human being could possibly remember. Well, I am not a normal human being. I have what is called "selective humourous photographic memory," which means I only remember the funny conversations. But rest assured, I remember them exactly. So, here goes. The truth and nothing but the truth. I hope it's not too boring.

Je Me Souviens

(I Remember)

My big entrance

On the day that I was born, it was crisp and cold. A bitchy blizzard had just deposited a foot of snow on the ground and another foot was on the way. They say it was so cold that day the rooster refused to come out to announce sunup. Later, they found him frozen in his coop.

My sisters were all gathered in the big, warm farm kitchen preparing the noon meal. As the wind howled outside, whipping the snowdrifts into piles of constantly shifting meringue, the women of my family bustled about inside, the cold a nasty rumour they'd heard of but wouldn't acknowledge. The fire burning in the stone hearth cackled like the Hag of Newfoundland. My mother had just taken a huge pork *tortière* out of the woodstove and set it on the table, a massive wooden monstrosity that stretched for more than ten feet, with built-in benches like a picnic table. It was capable of seating the entire brood, except for my sister Manon, who as they said in those days "wasn't quite right." She was about nine at the time and barely spoke, just sat on a stool in the corner of the kitchen playing an accordion all day long, which really must have been irritating. Luckily, by the time I was old enough to remember such things she had succumbed to rubella, at the tender age of thirteen.

Manon's accordion sang with longing and passion that day, and I imagine Maman humming to herself as she worked, the swell of her six-and-a-half-month pregnant belly barely noticeable under her considerable farmwife bulk. Maman was happy, they tell me, for she knew that I was to be her last child. The doctor said that at her age, forty-four, another child was inadvisable. They say that when she discovered she was pregnant once again, she declared "I don't care what it is. It can be a boy *and* a girl, for all I care." Little did she know.

It was a special day, because one of my brothers, Pierre, was about to turn ten. There was a family tradition in the Cole household where, at that age, the male children had to slaughter a pig with a sledgehammer while my father and the other boys watched. My father said he had brought this custom over from Scotland, but I think he just made it up.

The sight in the barn that day was a strange one. If you had been a shivering barn swallow hiding out in the rafters, you would have seen nine boys from the ages of eight to twenty-nine, wearing nothing but winter boots, kilts, and tams, all standing in a circle and drumming on their bare chests with their hands. In the middle of that circle, you would have seen a large sow snorting with fear in front of two little boys, one with a large sledgehammer. You would have seen my father, fifty-five at the time but still as strong as an ox, standing on a bale of hay in the corner of the barn playing a Scottish war tune on the bagpipes. He was shirtless, too, barrel-chested, with a sprawling red-gray beard and biblically fierce dark eyes. His nostrils shot steam into the air. Then you would have seen one little boy walk slowly over to another and take the sledgehammer from his hands. The boy with the hammer was my brother Gaston, who had become a man two years earlier, and the one taking the implement was my brother Pierre. Pierre brought the sledgehammer up over his head and I'm sure my father smiled, because nothing makes a Scot happier than horrible weather and the spilling of blood. The Cole boys began to drum harder and Angus's piping built in intensity. Death and manhood were imminent.

Meanwhile, back in the kitchen, Maman was clutching her distended belly. But it was not time! She called out to my sisters Fleur and Caresse to come to her. The pains came again, this time harder. I was impatient. Maman climbed atop the kitchen table with the help of the girls. She spread her legs, and straining to give me to the world, let out an awesome scream.

Back in the barn, my brother Pierre was still struggling to lift the massive sledgehammer. The pig had stopped squealing and looked up at him quietly. Suddenly the men heard the wailing coming from the kitchen. My father immediately put down his pipes and raced out of the barn, the boys following, struggling to keep up with the strides of my Braveheart father. The pig breathed a sigh of relief and trotted off to a corner of the barn to lie down in the straw. Pierre just stood there alone, holding the sledgehammer, confusion written all over his face. How do I know this, even though I wasn't there? A little bird told me. Pierre knew that this was to be his only chance; that, according to tradition, once the ritual had been interrupted, it could never be restaged. He knew he would never be a man now, which reminds me, this is my story.

Back with the womenfolk, a tiny newborn with more ego than life lay blue and shivering on the kitchen table. Fleur, who was twelve at the time, ran to the sink, grabbed a large knife, and severed the cord. Then she tied it in a bow, picked me up, and turned to my mother, who according to family lore waved her hand toward the pie. I think she was trying to say she was hungry and wanted a piece, but lucky for me, Fleur misunderstood, and slicing open a hole in the crust slid me into the warm, meaty interior. Colour immediately came to my cheeks and my eyes fluttered open. I would live.

At that moment, Papa and my brothers stormed in and raced over to the steaming pie. I had sufficiently recovered enough that I was now eating my bed. Breathing on my own, and already able to focus on a pretty face, it was decided that I would be all right. Everybody settled down to eat, carefully cutting around me. Everyone except Pierre, that is. He was so upset he refused to come in for lunch and spent the rest of the day inside the barn, crying. At least that's what the little bird told me. Then, as if my birth wasn't excitement enough, my cousin Tony, an altar boy at the village church, burst in to announce that the statue of the Virgin Mary was bleeding! Yes, gentle readers, on the day that I made my entrance, our Blessed Mother began to menstruate. I had no choice. I was born to rock.

Cornygirl

My earliest recollection is a very vague memory of my brother Pierre leaving home. I remember hearing a *clunkity-clunk* sound while lying in bed. Then I recall crawling over to the door and peeking into the hallway. Pierre was dragging a huge suitcase down the stairs. Our eyes met, and he put his finger to his mouth. "Shhhh." He continued on his way until I heard the door close behind him. Then I feel asleep on the floor, and when I awoke the next morning I was back in bed. No one ever mentioned Pierre again.

My second recollection is of a doll. It was a dried-out corncob with two buttons for eyes, a painted-on mouth, and Popsicle-stick arms and legs. I called her Cornygirl, and carried her everywhere I went. Cornygirl had been given to me by my oldest sister, Sister Monique Cole, of Our Lady of the Suffering Bleeding Heart of Jesus Convent. She was about thirty, had a mustache, short gray hair, and gams to die for, which she always kept hidden under that bloody habit. I was always telling her to hike it up a little. "Show some leg, Sister!" I'd say.

All my brothers and sisters hated Cornygirl. But Maman said that if anyone ever hurt little Cornygirl she would break their collarbone. My mother was always very specific about her threats. One day, I decided to make some clothes for

Cornygirl. The first thing I needed was material. I had my eye on my brother Yves's black leather jacket, which he had recently inherited from our older brother Felix. Felix had inherited it from Gaston, who had inherited it from Gilbert, and so on and so on. The massive jacket dwarfed Yves, who was eight years old at the time but was already starting to turn girls' heads. He thought he was pretty cool as he strutted around the house, but it looked ridiculous on him so I figured I was doing him a favour by stealing it. Even at that tender age, I was already putting other people's needs before my own.

The problem was, Yves never took off the jacket. Luckily, we both slept in the same bed, so one night, while Yves was sleeping, I gently slid the coat off him. Then, taking my sewing kit from under the bed, I stole up to the attic where I spent the rest of the night feverishly fashioning a smart nun's habit with the hem a few inches above the knee. Cornygirl looked fit to serve God with some flair. I finished just as the sun was coming up, and returned to the bedroom. Stashing the remains of the jacket under the bed, I tied myself up with some rope and began to scream.

Yves woke with a start, and soon the room filled with panicked members of my family. I told them that some man had broken into our bedroom, tied me up, and stole Yves's leather jacket. Incredibly enough, they believed me, and raced off to their own rooms to see if anything else was missing. When everyone had left except for Yves and our still-sleeping brother Davide, who could have slept through a succubus, he turned to me suspiciously.

"Where is my leather jacket?" seethed Yves.

"Your breath smells," I answered.

"Tell me where it is or I'll break your arm," he said.

"Just don't break my wrists. I have a feeling they're going to be my bread and butter in the future."

"I love what you've done with Cornygirl," came an annoying little voice from the corner of the room. It was Davide. He was holding Cornygirl and admiring her new leather ensemble. Yves grabbed the doll from his hands and glared at it.

"What's this?"

"Cornygirl's joined the church," I said. His response was a punch, and I went down like a sack of essence, leaving nothing but a wispy vapour trail. Somehow, Yves grabbed that vapour and squeezed it into an arm, which he twisted behind my back.

"I'm gonna make you my bitch," he snarled.

"Don't be possessive. I'm everybody's bitch." He hit me again, so I hit Davide. Davide began to cry, so I hit him again, then he hit me. Finally, Yves hit both of us. It dissolved into a melee until Maman came in to break it up. Yves told Maman that I had stolen his leather jacket and made an outfit for Cornygirl. I stuck to my original story, blaming the same mysterious man who had tied me up. Maman wanted to know what possible reason some man would have to break into a house, tie up a little boy, cut up a leather jacket, and make a dress for a doll. I said I had no idea, that I didn't understand the workings of the criminal mind. At that moment, Davide piped up once again to ruin everything.

"Look what I found," he said, fishing out the mutilated leather jacket from under the bed. That was enough proof for Maman. She ordered me to restore the jacket, and punished me by taking away Cornygirl for a week. When Maman left, Yves decided that her punishment wasn't enough.

"Here's the deal, little brother. You're my slave from now on. When I fart, I want you there to catch it. When I'm hungry, I want you to spoon-feed me. When I'm sore, I want you to rub me. You get it?"

"Deal," I said, and he let me up. I immediately stripped off his shirt and I got to work on his aching back. Some punishment.

As for Davide, I got even by planting a male physique magazine under his pillow and arranging for my older brothers to find it, thereby inventing "outing."

The legend of
loony lake

One summer day, out of the clear blue sky, my father asked me to go fishing. I hadn't really spoken to him in at least a year so I thought this was a marvelous opportunity to get caught up. We'd both been so busy, him raising a huge family and me wandering around in a fog talking to trees. We made a date for the following day.

We were going to Loony Lake, famous for both its small-mouth bass and its one loon, which was actually clinically insane. She was called Loony Loon and was rarely seen. All that was known about her was that she was crazy about hats.

Papa woke me at 4:30 A.M. with a glass of cold water thrown in my face. A Scottish alarm clock, he called it. We still hadn't gotten a new rooster. I dressed quickly in a smart blue seersucker suit, white tap shoes, a straw boater, and a jaunty cane, which I swung to and fro like Dick Van Dyke in *Mary Poppins*.

I clicked my way downstairs to the table where a bowl of gritty porridge awaited me. My father stood against the counter in his one-piece long johns, eating his porridge right out of the pot. He laughed when he saw me.

"We're going fishing, lad, not singing and dancing," he said.

"I'm just showing my respect for nature," I replied. "And the hat's to attract Loony."

"Well, you're a loon, all right." He laughed.

"That's why I'm so craaaaazy!" I said "crazy" like Paul Lynde, and Papa burst into helpless laughter. Everything was going great. My dad and I were clicking.

We grabbed our lunches and our fishing gear and headed off. It was about a forty-five minute walk through the woods. On the way, we chatted about recently elected Prime Minister Pierre Trudeau's declaration that the state had no place in the bedrooms of the nation. My father agreed, unless the "state" happened to be a beautiful blonde with big tits. We laughed our heads off.

When we arrived the lake was completely empty, except for a few people who seemed to have a lot of equipment of some kind about a hundred yards away. I was intrigued. Papa took his place on the shore and cast a line, but I couldn't stop looking at the strangers.

"Shake a leg, lad," said Papa. "What are you looking at?"

"I don't know. It looks like a movie camera."

"Why would there be a movie camera way the hell up here? Nothing here but bush." There was a splash and a cry from the group. Someone had dropped something into the water.

"Damn nuisance! Scare away all the fish."

"Papa, let's say I go over there and tell them to keep the noise down because we're trying to fish here in a quiet father-and-son manner."

"Sure, lad, and while you're there, see if you can bum some smokes from them." I trotted off to find out who they were, cursing the whole way as my tap shoes sank into the mud. When I got close, I saw that it was a man, a woman, and a movie camera—the Holy Trinity of filmmaking. I jumped in, tap shoes first.

"Hello, my name is Buddy Cole. I'm one of the simple

peasant children that dwell in the region. Perhaps my native talents can be of some service to you."

The man spoke first. He was of average size, soft like an academic, with a big black beard shot through with gray. He wore granny glasses from which two watery blue eyes peered out, and he had a bald spot shaped like Baffin Island.

"Hello, I'm Horace Charters, and this is my wife, Jane. We're making a documentary about Loony Loon for the National Film Board of Canada." For my American readers, the National Film Board of Canada is like MGM, only instead of musicals, they make documentaries.

Jane had graying, dishwater-blond, flyaway, shoulder-length hair, a washed-out patchy parchment complexion, and short, bitten-to-the-quick fingernails. Together they were an ad for *Sexless Naturalist* magazine. Jane spoke in a tiny voice.

"Hello." She cleared her throat. She tried again. Braver.

"Hello." Her voice cracked. She decided to change tactics. She stuck out her hand to shake mine and then changed it to the other one and then realizing that it was her wrong hand, she changed again and then let it fall to her side and subsided into muttering to herself. Okay, so they weren't Humphrey Bogart and Katharine Hepburn, but the National Film Board has won more Oscars than those two combined.

"Any luck with Loony?" I asked excitedly.

"No, we've been here for nine and a half days, and still no sighting of that elusive creature," he said. "We've tried everything to attract him. We tried radar, sonar—"

"Have you tried gaydar?" I suggested, using a term that hadn't even been invented yet. They just looked at me blankly. I had an idea.

"Why don't you just get a regular loon and make it crazy? You could put it in a big barrel and shake it, or force it to eat lots of mustard, or just tickle it until it goes out of its mind."

"But that would be fraudulent," protested Horace.

"Well, I heard that Nanook of the North was not an Eskimo at all. Just a heavily made-up Italian," I replied.

"No, that would never do," said Horace. "The reputation of the National Film Board is too illustrious to tarnish with trickery."

"I like your hat," blurted out Jane.

"Oh, yes, I wore it because. . . . Oh, sweet Jesus. The hat! Of course."

"What is it, peasant boy?" demanded Horace.

"It's the hat. Loony loves hats, you see. Get your camera ready, and watch this." I took my hat off and tipped it to an imaginary dance partner while attempting a soft shoe in the mud.

At that very moment, the surface of Loony Lake was broken and a streak of wet black and green shot into the sky. It was Loony. She flew up high, did a couple of loop-de-loops and then shot toward us. Inches from my face, Loony screeched to a halt, went "Blahhhh!", did a back flip in the air, sniffed her armpit, went "Phew!", and then shot back into the lake, singing "Tra la la." Jane captured the whole display on film—another NFB first. Once again, for my American readers, this is the Canadian equivalent of Sharon Stone flashing her beaver in *Basic Instinct*.

"How can we thank you?" said Horace.

"Just give me a film credit as loon wrangler," I said. They agreed and we said our good-byes. Well, Horace and I did. As far as I know, Jane is still there, trying to find the best way to say "Nice to have met you." When I returned to my father, he was fishing happily.

"Papa, I saw Loony Loon," I said.

"Oh, good." He couldn't have cared less. "Well, we're ready to go."

"What?"

"Caught our limit." He held up fifteen smallmouth bass to one large-mouth child.

"Which ones did I catch?"

He pointed to several beauties. "This one, this one, and this one."

"I'm a good fisherman, aren't I?"

"You take after your old man," he said. "Did you get any smokes for Papa from those people?"

"No, I forgot," I said. "Have one of mine." I took out two Export A's, lit them both, and handed one to Papa, just like Paul Henreid in *Now, Voyager*.

"Papa, do you think Loony Loon is happy?"

"Son," he said, gravely, "there are only three things you have to know. First, women are like trains. Don't jump on one until you know where she's going. Two, when you're in trouble with the law, or feel sick, or having money problems, go to a Jew. And three, when you're sitting in a bar, and some guy puts his hand on your knee, you just give him a good stiff punch on the jaw and tell him to fuck off."

"I agree," I said. We wandered home, arm in arm, eating Maman's peanut-butter-and-bacon sandwiches. Later that night we had a big fish fry. Papa allowed me my first sip of homemade mash, and I slept like a baby.

Mademoiselle saigon

As a boy, I loved to wander in the woods. It was the only time that I was ever alone. Maman would pack me a nice lunch of bacon sandwiches, a Pepsi, and a Vachon cake, and off I would go. My favourite part of the woods was called Pierre d'Etage, or Stage Rock. It was a natural granite formation with a proscenium arch and a thrust stage, the exact dimensions of Carnegie Hall. I loved to lie on that flat rock and just read the day away. Or sometimes, when the spirit overtook me, I would remove all my clothing and drape myself in moss, leaves, and branches, and dance to the music of the forest. I was Isadora Duncan's crazy country cousin, Duncan Adoresya.

Woodland creatures would often gather, mesmerized by my bending of modern dance conventions. After I finished, or more aptly collapsed to the ground in profound artistic exhaustion, they would chirp and chitter with approval. Then I would drink my Pepsi, read my book, and share my food with my audience. Sometimes the bigger animals would fight over the Vachon cake and rip each other to shreds. I know I should have stopped it, but you don't fool with Mother Nature. Besides, after the battle there was always lots of game to bring home, which made me a hero in Maman's eyes. That's why I still get misty-eyed at a cockfight. Of course, that's also where my parents met.

One day, the Muse overtook me in a way that she never had before and I couldn't stop dancing. My program began with an ode to decomposition, which the worms loved, followed by a savage satire on separatism, which most of the animals didn't get, and then finally my show-stopping "Dance of the Setting Sun," which brought them all back.

One part of me knew that the sun was actually setting and that I should head home before it got dark, but the other part of me didn't care. All I wanted to do was spin, and so spin I did, until the sun was totally swallowed up by the inky black night and the only light I had to dance by was owl eyes and fireflies. When the moon finally appeared in the sky, I lay spent on Pierre d'Etage. I drank the last of my Pepsi and sat up with a start. I realized that I had never been this far into the woods after dark. I felt a chill and quickly dressed.

Then I caught a very familiar scent. Frying bacon. Maman was cooking. I would just follow that, and soon I would be home, tucking into another bacon sandwich. I struck out in the direction of the smell.

It became stronger and stronger and even though the path didn't seem familiar, I just put that out of my head and continued. Suddenly, I saw a light and relaxed, but when I got closer I realized that it wasn't the farmhouse at all. It was a small shack. I had been tramping about these woods all my life, and never had I come across this particular abode. *Très mysterieux.* I went up to the window and looked in.

Bent over a woodstove was a strikingly handsome black man, about thirty years old, with no shirt on. I could see what looked like dog tags around his neck. To this day, I think I've never seen a finer sight.

As he turned from the stove our eyes met and I freaked out, tearing off into the woods. I heard the slamming of a door behind me and knew that he was in hot pursuit. I tripped over a branch and fell. He was on me faster than you could say "There's a girl in my soup!"

"Who are you?" he barked in strangely accented French.

"I'm Buddy Cole."

"What were you doing?" he said.

"I'm lost. I didn't mean anything." I began to cry. He immediately softened, picked me up in his arms, and carried me inside. My ploy worked. As he carried me I took the opportunity to read his dog tags. They said PRIVATE LINCOLN TOUSSAINT. A real ragin' Cajun. Inside, the cabin was very cozy. I felt faint with hunger as we passed by the sizzling pan of bacon. He laid me down on his unmade bed and then brought me a plate of bacon and eggs. I realized how famished I was and took it.

"Thanks. You're not from these parts, are you?" I asked.

"What gave it away? My bad French or the fact I'm a nigger?" he said. I'd never heard anyone say "nigger" before. It was so *TV*.

"Are you a Yankee?" I asked, excited by the sound of the word.

"I may be an American, but I'm no Yankee."

"Why are you living in the woods behind my house?"

"Ever hear of Vietnam?"

"It's my favorite show," I said.

"What about My Lai?"

"Is that the episode with the little girl running with her clothes burned off, or is that the one with everybody lying dead in the ditch?"

"The ditch one."

"That's my favorite show ever. That, and the *Flintstones* episode where they sing 'Way Out.' "

Lincoln's voice suddenly became spooky. "Sarge woke us up at 0400. The word had come down from HQ. So we rolled up a couple of fatties and killed a bottle of tequila. The junkies were already fixing. The sun was still passed out and already it was hotter than a bucket of cunt. I could smell slant blood in the air. We held our women tight."

"Women?" I asked.

"Our guns. When we came into the village, everybody was just getting up. The first person we saw was an old gook collecting firewood by the side of the road. I cut her head off because she looked at me."

"How can you even tell with Orientals?" I interrupted, being swept up in the racist bonhomie. He ignored me and continued.

"Then some little boy came out of a hut and began scream- ing when he saw the dead woman. Soon the place was filled with screaming gooks. Then, no one was screaming but me." He stopped and buried his face in his hands. I didn't like the self-pitying turn the tale had taken, so I decided to change the subject.

"What's that pretty doll?" I asked, pointing to a big doll propped up on a shelf.

"That's Pearl," he said.

I went over and picked her up. She was Oriental, very pretty, and was dressed like a Vietnamese peasant. She had a hole in her back, and I realized that she was a ventriloquist's dummy.

"Can you make her talk?" I asked.

"You'll have to ask her yourself," he said, taking the doll from my arms and putting his hand in her back.

"Pearl," I asked, "how are you?"

The doll's eyes snapped open, and a beautiful female voice with a delicate Vietnamese accent issued forth from the wooden head. Lincoln's lips never moved.

"As well as can be expected, for a girl who lost her entire family to American butchery." She looked accusingly at Pri- vate Toussaint. I couldn't believe it. She was real. More real than many people I'd met. I decided then and there that I wanted to be a ventriloquist.

"I found Pearl in what was left of the village we destroyed," said Lincoln. He looked haunted.

"Let me try," I said, grabbing for the doll.

"Sure. You put your hand in here to control the mouth."

"I know. I know." I was impatient. He begrudgingly handed me Pearl. I sat her on my lap and inserted my arm in all the way to my shoulder. I've only ever done that once since and it wasn't with a dummy, although he was pretty stupid. When I was snug and secure, I began to improvise an act, my lips moving frantically.

"So, I went to school today and boy was it stupid," I said in my own voice.

"Why was it so stupid, Buddy?" I made Pearl say in the voice of a Catskills comedian.

"Because the teachers are stupid and so are the students except for me." I turned expectantly to Lincoln.

"Well, what did you think?" I asked.

"That was the worst thing I've ever seen. I've seen more talent in a bug. You are the enemy of talent." And with that, he grabbed Pearl away from me and put her back on the shelf. Then, without saying another word, he lay down on the bed and promptly fell asleep. I was stung by his criticism, but not so hurt that I didn't climb into bed next to him and fall asleep with my face buried in his armpit. He owed me.

The next morning, I awoke first. Lincoln remained fast asleep, snoring. Remembering his jealous and uncalled-for attack on my talent, I tucked Pearl under my arm and scooted out the door. It was only fair.

I had no trouble finding my way home in the bright light of day. When I walked in, everyone was in the middle of breakfast. Luckily, no one had noticed that I was gone all night, so I just pretended that I was coming in from the barn. I told everyone that I had found Pearl in the woods and that I had decided to become a professional ventriloquist. Everyone ignored me, so I decided to give them a demonstration.

"Someone ask her a question," I said. Maman was the first to speak up.

"Do you do laundry?" she asked. Everybody laughed. I still didn't know how to throw my voice, so I made Pearl whisper the answer into my ear.

"She says that's a stupid question and refuses to answer," I bluffed. Maman looked stung.

"Don't get smart with your maman, little man," cautioned my father.

"But she's getting all my laughs," I whined.

"Then earn them," he said. I began again. But this time I had Pearl speak like Paul Lynde. That always got a laugh.

"Did you hear the one about the alien who married a human?"

"No, I didn't," I said to Pearl. Then I pretended that she whispered in my ear again. "Pearl says she's tired and the show's over." Everybody booed.

"You'll never be a ventriloquist," said Papa. "It takes years of practice. You don't have the patience." I knew he was right, but I still wasn't about to lose. I suddenly remembered that I'd recently learned hypnosis from the back of a cereal box. So I pulled out my big pocket watch and began swinging it to and fro in front of my hapless family.

"You are getting drowsy," I intoned. "Your eyes are getting heavy. You are very relaxed. Your eyes are closing. You are falling asleep." The whole room fell into a trance. I couldn't believe it. Every single member of my family was hypnotizable. What were the odds?

"When I snap my fingers, you will awaken, and you will be convinced that you have seen a world-class ventriloquist at the top of his game, and you will be energized by his performance." But before I could snap my fingers, the door burst open and Private Lincoln Toussaint charged in, wearing full metal jacket.

"Arrgghhh!!!" he roared, waving his M-16 in my face.

"Give me back my woman or I'll take your whole fucking family out!" He said "fuck." I didn't want a repeat of My Lai, so I tossed him the doll.

"Take her!" I yelled. "I'm through with women!" He grabbed me by the throat and lifted me into the air.

"Don't fuck with Uncle Sam, boy!" he roared, and threw me into the corner where I crumpled like a doll. He took Pearl in his arms and kissed her on the cheek. Her eyes opened and she spoke.

"You came for me, Lincoln. You must love me."

"You know I do, Pearl," he said, his eyes filling with tears.

"You had no choice that day in the village, did you?"

"I was just following orders," he said, weeping bitterly.

"I forgive you, soldier boy," said the doll. She touched his cheek with the tenderness of Jennifer Jones in *The Song of Bernadette*. Then, without firing a single shot, he raced out the door with Pearl under his arm. I freshened up at the sink and then turned to deal with my somnambulistic family. I snapped my fingers and they all woke up, applauding madly. Everyone crowded around to congratulate me.

"I feel energized by the performance!" said Papa. "Let's go feed some slop to the hogs." Everyone cheered and raced outside yelling "Chores!" The only person left was Maman, who was still sleeping. I pinched her awake.

"Oh, Buddy," she said. "I just had a dream that a Chinee woman was doing my laundry."

"We've all got to have our dreams, Maman," I said. Then I went upstairs to my room where I lay down with Cornygirl. Her rustic simplicity seemed worlds away from the sophistication of Pearl. But at least she let me do all the talking.

$\mathcal{I}$ learn the basics of math

We all went to the same school in town, a classic one-room brick schoolhouse for all grades from kindergarten through secondary level.

There were thirty kids in the class. Thirteen of them were from my family. Another seven were from the Poirier family, and four were from the Legault family. There were also the Croix triplets, a sexy Cree Indian boy named Merv Jackson, an American exchange student, and a mature student called Eleanor Hup who had returned to get her high school diploma at the age of seventy-three.

Merv and Ellie, as I liked to call her, were my best friends. We christened ourselves the Mod Squad. Eleanor was Julie, Merv was Link, and I was also Julie. We spent hours recreating the opening title sequence from the show.

Merv's parents were white former missionaries who had adopted him during the "Let's get an Indian child" heyday of the sixties. They were the first people I had ever met who recycled. Merv hated them.

Eleanor's children were all grown up and had left home, and her husband had recently died. Since his death, she had blossomed into a fireball of geriatric energy. She swam every morning from her house on Lac d'Eau to L'Isle des Memoirs and back again, and she dyed her hair green with pickle juice, so she gave off a vinegary odor. She liked me because I was funny, and I liked her because she smelled like vinegar, which was my favorite smell. The three of us were drawn to each other because we were different, but also because our desks were beside each other. A lot of life is just being in the right desk at the right time.

Our teacher was Brother Aloysius. He was a six-foot seven-inch hunched-over Jesuit monk in a black robe. His steely gray hair always looked slept-on and he sported huge black bat-wing eyebrows. He had rheumy eyes, hairy ears, and smoked constantly.

Brother Aloysius was always confused about which class he was teaching, so sometimes he would teach advanced math to the grade ones and read children's books to the grade twelves. I liked Brother Aloysius, and he liked me because I was bright and I loved to read. He would often lend me his rare literary treasures, like his collection of bathroom graffiti from ancient Abyssinia that in hindsight reminds me of Jeff Foxworthy's books. Or a tell-all biography of Jesus supposedly written by Jesus' "best friend," who was never once mentioned in the Bible, which I suppose was the reason behind the book's bitter tone.

On the last Friday of every month, Brother Aloysius gave everybody, no matter what grade, a quiz on religion. These tests were fifty percent of one's final grade, so they were very important. The questions were eccentric, to say the least, and the failure rate was high. The punishment for failure was the strap, which hung on the wall just inside the cloakroom. One Friday after a test, the Mod Squad was standing around in the school yard nursing our sore buttocks and having a smoke.

"What proof does he have that 'Kumbaya' was Jesus' favorite song?" I steamed. "Were rounds even invented then?"

"I know," chimed in Ellie. "Who says that Mary weighed a hundred and ten pounds?"

"Oh, good. I got that one right," said Merv.

"This abuse has got to stop," I declared.

"What are you going to do, Buddy? Go to the authorities?" asked Eleanor excitedly.

"No. I'm going to steal the test. I know where he keeps it."

"Where?" asked Merv.

"In that bust of the Virgin on his bookshelf. Tonight, we'll break into the school and get it," I said. They both agreed excitedly.

That night, the three of us gathered under the classroom window. Merv, an expert at breaking into buildings because his parents were always locking him out, jimmied it open. We clambered in as Ellie stood watch. Merv switched on his flashlight and pointed it toward the bust of the Virgin Mary. Her eyes stared at me with disappointment. First I had given her the curse and now I was going to steal from her. I put it down as a trick of the light. I reached inside, pulled out the test, and furiously made a copy. Then, careful to cover our tracks, we rejoined Ellie outside. The Mod Squad had struck again. Only this time for evil.

The next Friday, the three of us sat down at our desks and slyly smiled at each other as Brother Aloysius passed out the test. An hour later we were outside, sitting on the ground in victory, our bums free of pain. Maurice Legault, the sexy one, who was already shaving at eleven, staggered over to us rubbing his aching bum. I wished I had some ointment.

"How did you guys pass?" he asked.

"How much is it worth to you?"

"Fifty cents."

"Okay, at the end of next month, you give me fifty cents and I'll give you a copy of the test."

"But how do you get the answers?" he asked.

"God," I said, looking upward.

Maurice ran off to tell his nonsexy brothers about the offer.

I sensed that this would be very big. I turned to Merv and Ellie.

"How would you like to spend March break in Miami?" I asked.

Soon, our pockets jingled with cash. The next Friday, every single person in school passed. Brother Aloysius beamed with pride as he passed us back the marked tests. I sensed a certain melancholy, though, as he looked over at the forlorn strap.

The three of us conspirators gathered once again in the schoolyard. Our ill-begotten wealth burned a hole in our pockets. We all discussed what we would do with the money.

"I'm going to get my tattoo removed," said Eleanor. I had to agree it was a good idea. I had seen the large rendering of Popeye on her buttocks and no amount of spinach in the world could ever make me look again.

"I'm going to buy a gun and kill my parents," said Merv.

"I've heard that one before." I yawned.

"This time I mean it," Merv said defensively.

"Yeah, yeah. Blah blah blah," I responded.

"What are you going to do, Buddy?" asked Eleanor, ever the peacemaker.

"Nothing big. Maybe just freshen up my wardrobe a little," I said.

The next day, I pulled up to school an hour late in a cab. Everybody crowded to the window and stared jealously at me as I sauntered down the walk in a pair of five-inch platforms, yellow plastic pants, a pirate shirt, and a huge floppy brimmed hat. I walked into class and took my seat casually.

"Buddy, you are one hour late," said Brother Aloysius. "Do you have an explanation?"

"I'm sorry. Brunch was a disaster. Will five dollars cover it?"

Eleanor shot me a look. Merv looked angry. "Keep it cool. I have a gun," he said.

I looked down and saw a bulge in his pants. I gulped. I

looked over and saw another one. I gulped again. Brother Aloysius interrupted.

"Is there something you'd wish to share with the rest of the class, Mr. Cole?"

"Uh, yes," I said. "Brazil is actually larger than the continental United States."

"That's a lie!" shouted the American boy.

"Be quiet!" thundered Brother Aloysius. "Mr. Cole, would you please step outside with me for a moment?" I followed him outside. He wasted no time.

"I know you stole the test, Buddy. I found your fingerprints all over the bust of Mary. You didn't know that my Jesuit order specialized in forensics, did you?"

I gasped. I didn't know what to do. I wanted to blame the other two, but I was afraid of Merv, and Eleanor was an old lady. I decided to take another tactic before I hung Eleanor out to dry.

"The devil made me do it. I'm possessed!" I said. I vomited, tried to turn my head in a complete circle, and pissed on the ground. He didn't buy it. I looked through the window and saw Merv glaring at me. I noticed that the bulge in his pants was pointing toward me. And so was the other one. What to do?

"I did it!" I cried out. Brother Aloysius' eyes darted in the direction of the neglected strap. Moments later my plastic pants were down around my knees and I was bent over his desk being disciplined mercilessly in front of the whole class. The Virgin Mary's eyes beamed at me with pride. I was taking my licks. Later, when they found Merv's parents shot to death and lying in their own compost heap, I knew that I'd done the right thing.

The scaly angel

One winter, my father and my brothers and I went ice fishing. We headed out on the lake in snowmobiles. Claude and Jean-Claude cut a hole in the ice with a chainsaw. We gathered around with fishing poles. Everybody sat around passing a flask of Father's moonshine to each other. They passed it to me and I took a healthy swig. The fiery liquid burned my throat. A licentious warmth overtook my body. I leaped up and immediately stripped off my parka.

"Look, I'm Sally Rand!" I screamed. My brothers laughed and cheered me on.

"Take it off!" they yelled. I tore off my toque. For my American readers, a toque is a wool hat, much like the ones rappers sport today. Except in Canada, a toque is never cool.

Yves immediately launched into a lusty French folk song about an English tart with dentures, and soon everyone joined in. I began to dance. I danced the Dance of the Seven Outergarments—toque, coat, scarf, mittens, boots, long johns, and big, thick socks. All were peeled off to increasingly raunchy verses, sung at top volume, about that unfortunate English girl and all those fortunate French bikers. Soon I was naked on the ice. All of a sudden, my father blew up at me.

"Stop that! You're scaring the fish!" he yelled. I got so excited, I lost my balance and fell into the hole in the ice. My body slid down into the cold black depths of Lac d'Eau. I could see their arms reaching down for me as I plunged deeper, the light from the hole fading like a retreating star. Everything became colder and darker. I was dying and I knew it. Where was Cornygirl?

Then out of the still depths a pair of glowing, translucent eyes peered at me. It was a fish, but not just any fish. It was the biggest sturgeon I had ever seen. I looked in her eyes. They were loving. Well, for a fish. She swam up to me and offered me her fin. I took it and then she began to swim upward, dragging me along behind her.

Finally, we broke the surface. The strong arms of my brother Gilbert reached down and pulled me out of the water. He threw me onto the ice where I lay puking my guts out. I was quickly wrapped in an old quilt and taken home by snowmobile. Later that night, after a long restorative nap with Cornygirl, I padded downstairs, still wrapped in the quilt. My family was all gathered around the table eating. Everything seemed normal and I felt glad to be alive. Maman set a plate for me. I slid in next to my brother Yves. He squeezed my knee, happy to see me. I knew tonight that I would be receiving the back rub.

"What happened down there?" asked Fleur, her eyes moist with sisterly concern. Even though she was twenty-four years old, she still lived at home.

"Yeah," said Davide. "We thought you were dead. And then all of a sudden you came shooting out of that water like Esther Williams."

"There was a fish. . . ." I began. And then I saw something that froze my blood as cold as Lac d'Eau. Staring up at me from the serving plate was the remains of a giant fish. All that was left was the head, and the eyes that stared out at me were all too familiar. Loving. Crispy but loving.

At that moment, my father began to choke on a fish bone. He bolted up, clutched his throat, and fell forward onto the table, his eyes bulging and his face turning purple. Maman began to shriek, crying out "Angus! Angus!" over and over, clutching at his collar, and driving the bone deeper into his throat.

My brothers pulled her off him but no one knew what to do, as this was years before CPR awareness. Then before our horrified eyes, Papa choked to death.

As the girls comforted Maman, my brothers went into action. Daniel went to fetch the undertaker as the others laid Papa out on the sofa. Luckily, Maman had saved the caviar for me, so the day wasn't a complete disaster. I got a bowl and went upstairs where I found Yves crying in bed.

"Yves, don't cry," I said to him soothingly. "It takes away your masculinity." He didn't look up. I decided to try another tactic.

"Look what I found today." I pulled down my pants and showed him my first pubic hair, but he wasn't impressed, as he already had a bush you could do topiary with.

"How come you're not crying?" he sobbed.

"I'm crying inside. It doesn't age you that way. You know what's the best thing to do at a time like this? Help someone else out. My back's killing me."

"Papa just died!" he cried.

"I know. But I almost died today, too. We seem to be forgetting that."

"You're right," he said, damming up the tears. "Okay. Lie down and take your shirt off." And with that, he proceeded to give me the back rub of my life. What a day!

My life as
a laundry wench

After Papa died, everything changed. We had always been poor, but poor like the Waltons. Now we were poor like the Kettles. My mother was forced to take in people's laundry for money. I became her little laundry slave. I was in charge of the men's underclothes. Every day I was up to my flashing hazel eyes in one-piece long johns with trapdoors, boxer shorts, spaghetti-strap undershirts with big sweat stains, smelly T-shirts, and stinky woolen socks. None of the other brothers would do the job and the girls were considered too delicate for the task, which was absurd if you'd seen some of my sisters. So it fell to me. For some reason I never complained.

One day Maman took all the children to town to see Madame Levesque's goiter. She was showing it for five minutes at a time in her sitting room at ten cents a person or fifteen cents for sets of twins or triplets. Since my family had sets of both, my mother couldn't turn down the bargain. She may have been a poor widow but she still liked to have a good time. There hadn't been a lot of joy in our house since Papa's death and besides, Madame Levesque was reputed to serve a lovely meal with the viewing. The thing was, no one had ever been known to eat anything, but I knew that this wouldn't be a problem with my family. After you've eaten in a pig barn, you can eat anywhere. And for us, five minutes was more than enough time to wolf down a free meal.

I was not allowed to go, as my mother was still angry at me for an incident the week before. She had started dating again and was very nervous about an upcoming evening out with a recently widowed farmer. So I offered to make her up. I'd been making up my sisters for a few years by then with varying results. My greatest triumph had been to completely hide my sister Claudette's hair lip through the artful use of lipstick, lip liner and pine gum. Now she's a hooker in Montreal. But that's another story.

My mother was a hard case, though. Almost sixty at the time and showing every mile, she had never worn makeup before, so I had to be careful. I decided to give her the best features of all my favourite stars. I gave her Elizabeth Taylor's cat eyes in *Cleopatra*, Marilyn Monroe's rosebud mouth in *Niagara*, Joan Crawford's arched eyebrows in *Mildred Pierce*, and Anne Francis's mole in *Bad Day at Black Rock*, though with my mother it was more a question of covering up moles than drawing them on. She ended up looking like Edith Massey, in *Polyester*, and the farmer offered her a prize stud swine for a roll in the hay. Needless to say she was mortified and blamed me. The funny thing was, she did come home the next morning with the pig.

So off they went, leaving me alone in the house as punishment. At first I was depressed because I had dreamed of seeing the goiter for weeks. But then it dawned on me. I was alone. For the first time in my life, I was alone in the house. My blues instantly disappeared and I was instead filled with a feeling of exhilaration. The house, which usually closed in on me like an iron maiden, now seemed spacious and huge with possibilities. What would I do first? Like most boys, the first thing I thought of doing was choreographing a dance. I rushed to the living room and was in the midst of pushing all the furniture against the wall when there came a knock at the door. There stood a vision covered in sweat and copper dust, holding a bundle of dirty clothes. It was Romeo Gouter, the sexiest boy in the mine. Romeo was actually a man, nineteen years old and considered a bit of a roué because he ironed his curly hair flat. I thought he was super-fine.

"Where's your maman?" he asked.

"She's taken everyone to see Madame Levesque's goiter," I answered.

"Oh, yes," he said. "I saw it three days ago. I was the first in line." I was very impressed. Not only gorgeous, but morbid, too.

"So are you alone?" he asked.

"Yes," I said. "But I am still authorized to take your laundry." I flushed hot. Authorized? Who did I think I was? The R.C.M.P.? For my American readers, the R.C.M.P. are those Canadian cops that Disney bought.

"Okay," he said. "Here." My hand trembled as he handed me his precious garments. It was mid-July and the heat was intense. Sweat glistened on his brow and fell in rivulets into his sexy brown eyes.

"Sure is hot, eh?" he said, the consonants in his speech heavy with straight intent, the vowels dancing with gay possibility. I said nothing. I just stared at his belt buckle, which announced him as a regional curling champion.

"I forgot one thing. I hope you don't mind." He undid his curling buckle and his pants fell to the floor. Quickly stepping out of them, he casually slid his boxer shorts down to his ankles. His thick, uncut penis swung out. I looked at it. It was like looking right into the sun.

"Ever seen one that big before?" he asked. Actually I had. Many times. My brothers were all bigger than him, but I already knew a lot about the male ego, so I lied and said I hadn't. He smiled with pride and scooped the warm boxers up with his foot. He stuck the foot with the underwear hanging off it in my face. It smelled like fresh bread. I reverently took it and placed it gently on the pile on the floor. Then, mustering up all my self-control, I turned to him.

"It should be ready by tomorrow. I'll take care of it personally myself. Come by around noon."

"Okay," he replied, his voice husky. We just stared at each other. This was as far as I was willing to take it. I had what I wanted. Then he slipped his pants back on, very slowly did his belt up, and went to the door. The window of opportunity had passed. He paused.

"See you tomorrow." I closed the door and watched through the window as he walked down the path to the road. He looked even more beautiful from behind, which was something I didn't understand then, but would become clearer to me later in life. Then I got his underwear and began to dance.

Opportunity knocks

There's a magazine in Quebec called *Allo Police*. It's a tabloid filled with horrible pictures of people who have been murdered, and lurid tales of how they got that way. My sister Jeanne and I were obsessed with it and poured over it constantly. Maman didn't approve of the magazine, though, so we had to hide our few copies in the attic.

One cold spring morning we were up there reading a story about a teenage boy who'd bludgeoned his grandparents to death with a hockey trophy, when I spotted an ad seeking contestants for "The Prettiest Feet in All Quebec Pageant." All you had to do was send in the best picture of your feet, and the twelve most beautiful submissions would be whisked off to Montreal to compete in the pageant in July. The winner would receive one hundred dollars and tour the province for the summer in sandals. It was open to men and women of any age, as long as you had feet.

Well, I knew what I had. Whenever I visited people's homes, they would often ask me to take off my shoes and socks. It was fate. I immediately told Jeanne of my plans to enter the contest, and she agreed to help me. She always did. Jeanne wasn't the swiftest of my sisters, but what she lacked in brains she more than made up for in devotion. We decided to enlist the aid of another sister, Pascal, who was a bit of a photography whiz. Pascal was one of the oldest girls, and even though she was in her late twenties by then, she had never left home, either. This might have been because she was close to seven feet tall, or it might not. I never really asked her. You see, there were so many siblings in my family, there were some I barely knew.

After introducing myself to Pascal, I discovered that she was very nice. I felt bad that I'd run from her in fear so often when I was little. She also appeared to be a very talented photographer and had a large portfolio, mostly pictures of pigs, especially their feet. I couldn't believe my luck. Pascal insisted we shoot in the barn. She said that the light coming through the cracks in the wall diffused by all the dust in the air would be magical. I enlisted Jeanne in gathering the props and giving me a thorough pedicure. Finally, we were ready.

We were making our way to the barn on the day of the shoot when we were confronted by my brother Guy. Ever since Papa died, Guy had changed. Before, he was a happy-go-lucky person who enjoyed hunting and fucking. Now he went around muttering to himself and occasionally exploding for no apparent reason. The salient features of my brother Guy were his magnificent chest and his large ears, which grew red when he was angry. They were bright red now.

"Where are you going?" he demanded.

"What business is it of yours?" I replied, trying to sound like a Shakespearean sentry with attitude.

"I need you to help me with Betty. I need you to help me shoe her." Betty was an old sow who lived on her own in a special pen built by Guy. "Betty's going to make us rich. I'm going to rent her out, and let people ride her once around the yard for fifty cents."

"That is the most ridiculous thing that I have ever heard. Now, if you'll excuse us, we have a photo shoot with my feet."

"Why are you such a freak?"

"I will remind you that even though I possess a composure well beyond my years, I am still officially just a kid."

"A little faggot kid, from what I hear." Yves must have squealed.

"Better a faggot than a cauliflower bush on fire."

He swung at me, screaming like some Japanese banzai warrior, and caught me hard across the jaw. I went down. The girls scattered. Well, Jeanne scattered. Pascal just took one step back. I jumped up and hit him hard in the stomach. He doubled over in pain and I grabbed his ears and hung on for dear life. He slammed me into the barn door and I thought I heard a rib cracking. I pictured myself with an incredibly sexy bandage across my chest like Clint Eastwood in *The Beguiled*. Guy took advantage of my daydreaming and elbowed me hard in the ribs. But sadly, nothing broke. Then the fight disintegrated into mayhem. Finally, Pascal pulled him off me and Guy ran away, muttering to himself. I was disappointed to find that I was still conscious. People only get knocked out in the movies.

Assessing the damage, we discovered my entire body was covered with bruises, except for my feet, so I insisted the shoot go on. It hurt like blazes to move but we fixed up a system of ropes and pulleys to maneuver me.

With the subtle use of props gathered by Jeanne, my feet were transformed into works of art: my feet lying on a bed of bright green moss like some succulent sashimi; my feet wrapped in birch bark and bacon; my feet *en pointe*, with water running down the arches like a waterfall to a bed of colourful rocks and painted toes; even my feet nestled gently around a sleeping piglet.

When Pascal developed the pictures, I couldn't believe it. They were breathtaking. The challenging circumstances had given them a wartime urgency. It was impossible to pick one, but in the end we chose a shot of my feet resting on white sand late in the day that made them look like the Pyramids at dusk. We sent it off and waited. Time passed very slowly.

Oddly enough, Guy's Riding Pig scheme had taken off and people came from everywhere to ride Betty around and around a tiny circle at the end of a rope held by a bare-chested Guy. The attraction was so popular it threatened to topple Madame Levesque's goiter from the top of the charts. I had to admit, Guy had a fabulous chest. It made you forget about the ears. I think that was the real reason people came to ride the pig.

Then one day, a man in a bowler hat came to the door and told Maman that I had been chosen as a finalist in the Prettiest Feet in All Quebec Pageant, and that I should come with him. His name was Ronald Colman, and like the old movie star, he possessed the same kind of old-world style. He had thick salt-and-pepper hair, a big mustache that curled at each end, vivid blue eyes, and he spoke French with an English accent.

My mother was suspicious, but one less child was one less mouth to feed, and besides, the prize money was a big incentive. I begged Maman to let me go, reminding her of how much I ate. That did it. And so, with very little adieu, I packed a couple of smart outfits, grabbed Cornygirl, and said good-bye to whoever happened to be in the room at the time.

Charles in charge

There was a big yellow limousine idling in the driveway outside. Ronald opened the door and I got in. Sitting in the back was a woman with shoulder-length gray hair, a grim mouth, and large man's hands in which, for some reason, she held a gray stone. Her name was Dianne Leblanc, and even though she had been introduced to me as the chauffeur, she rode in the back while Ronald drove.

The entire drive to Montreal, Ronald and I chatted and played "I Spy." We spied a lot of trees. I tried to engage Dianne in conversation, but she was completely oblivious to my charms. She just sat there playing with that stupid rock. It's not like it was a jewel. If I had a jewel of any kind, I'd probably just hold it all the time, too. But a gray rock? I finally fell asleep dreaming of buried treasure and pirate rape. The next thing I knew, Ronald was gently shaking me awake. We had arrived.

We walked into the foyer of l'Hotel de Luxe. I couldn't believe the luxury. Mirrored walls, a chandelier, shag carpet. I thought it was the Taj Mahal, although since it was the first hotel I'd sleep in, a cot in a drunk tank would have impressed me. Ronald said he'd check me in and I giggled. I felt so adult. Like the first time I shaved my legs.

"Here's your room key and the key to your minibar. Your bag has already been taken care of. I'll have the concierge give you a wake-up call at eight. Everything begins at nine. If there's anything you need, I'm in Room 717." I was breathless. There was so much to absorb. Your own key, something called a minibar, wake-up calls. It was too much.

"I'll see you tomorrow, then," I chirped brightly.

"Yes, well, good night, then." Ronald turned and walked down the hall toward the elevators. I lingered, looking at some hotel literature, and when he disappeared around the corner, I slunk out the front door and into the dirty white night of downtown Montreal.

I went into the first bar I saw that looked gay, called Bar Apollo. Now, I was not yet legal drinking age, but I was armed with a fake ID from my brother Yves, who wanted me to buy him some skin magazines of women lactating. I was always amazed that my brother knew what he wanted at a young age, whereas I still don't know. With me, it depends on when you ask me. One moment I'm completely into skinheads who want to beat me up, and the next moment I just want a flavoured coffee with a theater administrator in a quiet café.

The bouncer took one look at my angelic underage face and let me right in. It's true what they say about gay life. It's easy to get in, but it's a bitch to get out. I made my way through a sea of sissies to the bar. Then I couldn't think of anything to order. On the farm, everyone just drank homemade liquor. It didn't have a name. Sometimes it was made from potatoes, other times it was from corn. One time it was from mud. As long as it kicked your ass, that's all that mattered. I suddenly remembered a James Bond movie I'd seen once in town, where Sean Connery ordered something called a martini. So I did, beginning a love affair that continues to this day.

Clutching my cocktail, I made my way to a corner where I could observe the room. It seemed like everybody had a mustache except for a young guy in the opposite corner, sitting on a stack of beer cases. He was a little older than me, with a muscular body, and was drumming madly along to the song "Taking Care of Business," by Bachman-Turner Overdrive. His long dirty-blond hair was wet with sweat, and whipped around his neck as he drummed. A group of eight queens stood nearby, pretending not to look at him. The drummer didn't have to pretend not to notice them because, bless me Mary, he was looking right at me, sporting the biggest grin I had ever seen on a non–movie star. I was completely enraptured.

I immediately started playing air fiddle, and jigged over to him, bumping into guys and spilling their beers. He laughed and began to drum more elaborately, using his chest as a snare and his stomach as a kick drum. Realizing that the fiddle was going nowhere, I threw the air instrument down and bent over, offering my own buttocks as the high and low toms. He began drumming madly on my ass, coaxing sounds out of my bum flesh that even Ringo couldn't achieve. The song ended, and we began to speak.

"We should start a band," I said.

"Yeah, we could call ourselves The Body Beat," he said. I laughed at his bad joke and took the opportunity to fall against his chest with one last drumroll.

"My name is Rolly Mec," he said. He held out his hand to shake, but, still caught up in the rhythm, I hit it, thereby inventing the high five.

"My name is Buddy Cole."

"We have an audience." Sure enough, the eight queens had tightened their circle around us. We were surrounded.

"You're right," I said. "Let me see if I can't do anything about that." I bent over and clenched my ass cheeks, and aiming my bum in the direction of the judgmental gay octopi, let out the most horrific-smelling pork fart that I could muster. They scattered.

"Whoa!" said Rolly, impressed. "That worked." An hour

later we were back in my hotel room, smoking a big honey oil joint given to me by Yves. Rolly lay stretched out on the bed, still shirtless, watching TV. I got right to the point.

"So, did you lose your shirt?"

"I don't own one. I used to have a shirt, then about a year ago, I lost it, and never got another one."

"But don't you need one for work?"

"I'm a lifeguard." That gave me an idea. I immediately plunged my face into my martini.

"Help me! I'm drowning! Shark!" I flailed about, shrieking.

Rolly, caught up in the madness, grabbed me by the hair, pulled me out of the vodka in the nick of time, and dragged me up onto the bed. Then he tilted my head back and proceeded to give me mouth-to-mouth resuscitation. In his life-giving air I could taste the building blocks of life—alcohol and chlorine. My eyes fluttered open. Then I, always a bitch for verisimilitude, turned my head to the side and puked once, ladylike, onto the coverlet. He wiped my mouth, and began to kiss me wildly. I kissed him back, and soon we were engaged in the oldest act known to gay man. I had fooled around with plenty of boys in my youth, but this was the first time I ever knew what it was like to be a woman, if you know what I mean. Cut to the drapes blowing in the open window, and fade.

The next morning I woke up with a start. It was nine o'clock. I must have slept right through the wake-up call. I could just make it. Rousing Rolly, we both quickly dressed, and I ran down to the lobby only to discover that everyone had already left, with the exception of Ronald Colman, who looked furious.

"I've held the limo for you. Hurry up or Dianne will leave." We got into the car. Ronald drove in silence as I sat in the back with Dianne. No one spoke the whole trip. Finally, we got to the theater and went in through the stage door. As we walked down the long dark corridors, the only sound was of our heels clicking on the concrete floor. When we got to my dressing room, Ronald shut the door and turned to me.

"That was quite a display you put on last night!"

"What?" I sputtered.

"I was there. I saw the whole shameful performance. My seven friends and I were mortified."

"What, you were one of them? I didn't notice you."

"Youth never notices Age. That is the way of the world, my young friend. How do I know that? Because I am Age!" he said grandly. He really lived up to his namesake. I had nothing to say, so he went on.

"Your mother entrusted you to me. What would she say if she knew that I let her young boy go out to a gay bar in Montreal and be used as a human drum by a ruffian? She would say that I let down not only her but also myself, the pageant, the people of Quebec, and Her Majesty the Queen." He paused and I could see his mood immediately switch over.

"Now, go out there and win! Even though I'm officially neutral, my money's on you." Then, as if he had said too much, he abruptly left. I had to pull myself together. My psyche had just taken an emotional beating and who knew how it had affected my feet! The stage manager took me to where a televised press conference was already in progress. There were twelve chairs, twelve microphones, and twelve footstools, all of them occupied by a contestant, save for one. The other contestants were all displaying their feet on the footstools. I could see that my chair was at the other end of the dais and the only way to get there was to walk in front of everyone. I made my way awkwardly over to the chair.

"Excuse me, excuse me, excuse me, excuse me, excuse me, excuse me, excuse me, excuse me, excuse me, excuse me, excuse me," I said. I reached my chair and sat down. I removed my shoes and socks and put my feet up, causing a ripple in the crowd.

The contestant from Sherbrooke, a trucker with big, muscular, hairy feet and a long black beard, was in the midst of answering a question about the merits of skin-softening lotion versus pumice. Then another question was asked of the contestant next to me, a very pretty, very young, porcelain doll of a girl.

"Contestant from Rouyn-Noranda, when you have a blister, do you burst it or leave it alone?" asked a judge.

"I've never had a blister," the doll-child said. The crowd *ahhed*. Her feet twinkled.

"Contestant from St. Hubert sur la Lac?" said a judge. I looked attentive.

"You are on a train going seventy miles an hour toward a bridge spanning a thousand-foot gorge. Five hundred feet before the train reaches the bridge, you realize that you left your favourite shoes at home. How much time do you have to decide to jump before you reach the gorge?"

"I would never take the train," I replied. The room erupted with laughter and one of the judges clapped with joy. I was already a cinch for the congeniality award.

After the press conference was over, we all retreated to our dressing rooms for a light lunch and an Epsom salt footbath. Following lunch was the talent portion of the show. I had prepared a scene from Michel Tremblay's *Les Belles Soeurs*, performed by my ten toes. For my American readers, and most of my Canadian ones, too, it's a play about a group of sisters in Quebec who sit around a kitchen table smoking. I was in my room running lines when Ronald burst in.

"Buddy, you have a telegram. It's from home. Everyone's watching and wishes you luck."

"Oh, that's nice. I can just see them all gathered around the picture window of the TV store. Pascal watching a television on the second floor, and Maman crying because she thinks I've been shrunk and put into a little box."

"They're proud of you."

"I know, and I didn't do anything for it. I was just born with these feet," I said humbly.

An hour later, I was backstage, waiting to go on. I heard Ronald's voice over the sound system, announcing the next act. It was a middle-aged East Indian woman who had transformed her feet into cobs of corn, peeling off each leaf to snake-charmer music. Each toe had a ring around it, and the big toes were painted up like cobras with their hoods flared. It was a real showstopper. My only hope was that the judges were racist.

Ronald's voice announced me next. Since I was performing one of *la belle province*'s treasures, I had Quebec nationalism on my side, which is *formidable*. I sat down and placed my feet inside the tiny proscenium arch. The set consisted of a tiny round table covered with tiny bingo cards. My toes—or shall I call them my cast?—took their places on the tiny kitchen chairs. The drama began.

About two minutes into the scene, Baby Toe forgot her lines and had to be prompted by Big Toe on the other foot. She became very defensive and a scuffle ensued. Big Toe was pushed and fell to the ground. The scene had to be called to a halt. It didn't look good.

The final portion of the pageant was called "Up Close and Personal." This was where the judges finally got to see what our feet were really made of. One by one the judges, each armed with a magnifying glass and calipers, came around for a personal inspection. I placed my feet on the black pillow. A spotlight clicked on. My feet gleamed like ivory. The first judge approached. He leaned in close, and raised his magnifying glass over my heel. Some dark thought crossed his mind, and a tiny "Hmmm" escaped his lips. He took his finger and pressed it into my arch. This was the response test, very crucial. The dent in the foot stayed there.

"Hmmm, very slow response time." He moved down further, to the ball of the foot. What looked like nothing to an unmagnified eye was, under the truth-telling glass, revealed to be a tiny bruise. This was not good. Ronald looked at me with disappointment. I suddenly regretted the indulgences of the night before. I made a vow to change my ways, and then I completely forgot about it.

There was only one last chance—my toenails. I knew they were flawless, but would it be enough to snatch me from the jaws of defeat? The magnifying glass took in the toes.

"Magnifique! Mes compliments au chef!" gasped the judge. The other judges crowded in and cooed. I let out my breath. I was reprieved. But would it be enough to win?

All the contestants gathered onstage. Ronald read the name of the three finalists—the little girl, an incredibly old woman, and *moi*. He couldn't help but smile a little when he said my name. The three of us held hands. The little girl's hand was clammy, the old woman's was as dry as a snake. Then he announced the second runner-up. It was the little girl.

"Congratulations," I said ingenuously.

"Fuck you," she replied as she slipped into the third place shoes: green plastic flip-flops.

"The next name called will be the name of the first runner-up," said Ronald. "Now, remember this is an important position, for in the event that the winner can no longer fulfill his or her duties, the first runner-up will become the Prettiest Feet in All Quebec." The room was eerily silent.

"And the first runner-up is . . . Charles Buddy Cole!" he bellowed. I smiled, but without using my eyes.

"Welcome the new Prettiest Feet in All Quebec, Madame Louise Bernard!"

The other contestants buzzed around her, pushing me aside. Madame Louise slipped into the white leather open-toed sandals of the winner and commenced her victory walk, as I sullenly donned my second-place brown rubber sandals. But the excitement proved too much for the old dear. Just before she reached the end of the ramp she slipped and twisted her ankle. She fell to the ground, the swelling immediately apparent. Ronald ran to her aid, helping her up as the crowd looked on in concern. I tried to hide my excitement. The television cameras sucked up the incredible drama and spewed it right back into the faces of the devouring public.

The next day, it was in all the papers. Pictures of the swollen ankle were everywhere. Every *boîte*, *depaneur*, and *l'office* was filled with people debating what to do. I stayed out of it, except for one quote attributed to me in the newspaper *Le Devoir* that I don't remember making—"At her age, it takes forever to heal. My mother, who's older than Methuselah but still younger than Madame Bernard, once had a bruise on her upper arm that lasted for five years. Besides, septicemia could set in, travel up to her heart, and kill her." I didn't know what septicemia was, but it sure sounded good.

Soon, the entire province was swept up in the debate, and a referendum was called, thereby inventing separatism. On April 12, Quebecers went to the polls to determine who should be the Prettiest Feet in All Quebec. The tally was 49.5 percent for Madame Louise Bernard, and 50.5 percent against. Allegations of political chicanery flew. Ronald was accused of fixing the results, and calls for a second referendum went up. Nobody trusted anyone. Brother turned on brother, mother turned on daughter, and fag turned on faghag. It was a dark chapter in Quebec's history.

Then, suddenly, Madame Louise died. Septicemia, apparently. Who knew? And with that, I ascended to my rightful place upon the throne.

La tour

The morning after my coronation, I woke up late to the sound of Ronald knocking on my hotel room door.

"Buddy, the train's pulling out in ten minutes. Hurry."

"Oh, just a minute. I just want to say good-bye to my hotel room," I called out. I turned to Rolly, who was pulling on his Levi cutoffs. He flipped his hair back with his hand.

"I must go, Rolly. My reign has begun. Everything's different now. I can't be with you anymore. I belong to all of Quebec now." I gave him one last kiss on the cheek.

"You have a great ass," said Rolly. "Tight as a snare." And with that, he leaped out the window, fell five stories, rolled off a parked car, and popped up, completely unharmed. Then he looked down and found a quarter. My lucky Rolly.

Five minutes later I was standing on the back caboose of a CN train pulling out of the station, headed for a whistle-stop tour of the province. A crowd had gathered to see us off, mostly hard-core foot fetishists and separatists. Our first stop was Trois-Rivières, where the mayor presented me with the key to the city, and the key to his hotel room, which I declined. I gave a brief speech about foot hygiene, kissed a baby, tasted a woman's apple pie, played sax in a school yard, and threw the opening pitch of a baseball game. Then it was on to Quatre-Rivières, where I did the exact same thing, except it was a rhubarb pie this time. And so on, and so on, and so on.

The tour went on like this all through the summer. I vowed to be the best Prettiest Feet winner ever. I threw myself into my duties and responsibilities, never complained, never explained.

Ronald and I were becoming very close and sometimes late at night, as the train sped through the countryside, we would meet in the club car and plan the next day's activities over drinks. I would sit there with my ginger ale and he would down tumbler after tumbler of Scotch, never showing a thing. Sometimes these nights stretched into days, and these days stretched into clichés. It was the best of times, it was the worst of times. You get the picture.

One night, Ronald was very deep in his cups, and I sensed that his British reserve had thawed enough for me to ask some probing questions.

"Did you ever shoot a cannon before?" I asked him. Ronald looked sad. I sensed that he had. He seemed defeated and I felt my heart swell with tenderness. Underneath all that English reserve, he was completely human.

"By the way, why were you even at that gay bar in Montreal? You're not gay."

"No, but most of my friends in the pageant industry are," he replied.

"What's with you and Dianne, then?"

"Dianne and I are lovers."

"But you're handsome."

"Well, you wouldn't know to look at her, but underneath that shapeless chauffeur's uniform, she has a ripping bod," he said, smoothing his mustache.

"Why doesn't she drive when she's supposedly the chauffeur?" I asked.

"Well, she used to. In fact, she loved driving. She was a

cabdriver in Montreal. One day, while heading down St. Catherine's Street, some hopped-up punk threw a rock through the driver-side window. It hit Dianne in the head and she went unconscious and drove straight into a doughnut shop, killing three people. Dianne was fine, but she never drove again. And to this day, she will not touch a doughnut."

"Did they ever find the guy who threw the rock?" I asked.

"No, he disappeared from the face of the earth."

"Is that the same rock she carries around all the time?"

"Yes. She wants to return it, in a manner of speaking." The way he said this spooked me, so I excused myself graciously and tottered off to bed.

A classy return

Traditionally, the tour ends in the winner's hometown, and so it came to pass that one fine end of summer's day we pulled into the tiny train station of St. Hubert sur la Lac. I had dressed up for the occasion in my best suit and the white leather sandals. I couldn't wait to see everyone. The train came around the heavily wooded bend and began to slow down. I could see the station. Ronald appeared beside me with my packed bag.

"Well, cheerio then." He handed me the bag and pushed me off the still-moving train onto the platform.

"What are you doing?" I yelled.

"It's better this way. I hate good-byes." The train began to pick up speed.

"I'll never forget you," I screamed. Ronald didn't reply. He just ducked inside the train and disappeared. I looked around expecting to see my family, but the platform appeared empty except for a large oak tree and a ficus benjamina bush. That's funny, I thought. Ficus benjamina doesn't grow wild here. The stationmaster must be gay.

I picked up my bags with a sigh and pointed myself in the direction of home. After a few steps, I thought I heard something rustling behind me, so I turned around. The oak tree and ficus benjamina seemed to have moved. I continued. I heard the same sound as before. I spun around abruptly. All vegetation came to a standstill except for the oak tree and ficus benjamina, which were shaking as if in a breeze. I went over to the tree and made as if to pee against the trunk. Suddenly a branch clubbed me across the head and a familiar deep voice called out. It was Pascal. The ficus benjamina jumped up to reveal my sister Jeanne.

"I'm a bush," she said and fell about laughing. Pascal smiled and hugged me. Her bark scratched like stubble.

"We thought we'd surprise you," she said.

"Well, you did. I must say, your costumes are very sophisti-cated. You've come a long way since you did my feet."

"Jeanne is a costume genius." We looked over at my slow sister, who was still laughing.

"I'm a bush," she said again and began to laugh even harder.

"Let's go home, Jeanne," said Pascal.

"A bushy bush!" Jeanne shrieked.

"Can we take the long way home?" I asked. "I want to see some of my old haunts."

"Sure," said Pascal. "It's your homecoming." On the way, I was overwhelmed by memories as I visited each special place—the tree where I blew Johnny Chevalier, the rock where I blew Maurice Legault, and the brook where I blew Bobby Bleu. These were the memories that lit the corners of my mind.

By the time we came upon the house, it was late and the sun was setting. We walked up to the door and opened it. The noise that blasted us was tremendous. A wild party was in progress. I noticed a torn banner hanging from the ceiling. It said WELCOME HOME, BUDDY! My party-loving family just couldn't wait. I know how that is. Let's just say I'm not the one you leave alone with the coke.

The first person I saw was Maman. She was passed out in

the corner on a kitchen chair. I walked up to her. Her lip was charred from a cigarette that had burned out in her mouth hours earlier. I kissed her there and her eyes fluttered open. Well, came unglued.

"Welcome home, son," she croaked. Then she closed her eyes and passed out again. Poor old girl, I thought. Well, at least she wasn't pregnant again.

No one noticed that I was there. I could see Marie Claire rubbing balloons against her chest and placing them on the wall. Claude and Jean-Claude were arm wrestling each other shirtless across the kitchen table, a couple of neighbourhood sluts hanging over them like Spanish moss. Christianne, who had blossomed into a radiant beauty in my absence, was bent over the stove. I went over to her, actually pushing aside family members who were too drunk to recognize me.

"Buddy," she cooed, and swept me up in an embrace. My brother Guy hove into view. His ears were flushed.

"Sorry I couldn't pick you up at the train station, little brother, but my pig broke down. Ha ha. That's funny, eh? My pig broke down. Pigs don't break down. They fall down. Isn't that true, Bobby? It is Bobby, isn't it? You've been away so long. I hear you even forgot how to speak French."

"I missed you, too."

"Look, Buddy, I baked a *tortière* for you in honour of your return," sang Christianne. She pointed toward the kitchen table where the remnants of a massive meat pie lay.

"It's gone," I whined.

"I'm sorry. No one could wait," she said, shooting a dirty look at Guy. Suddenly someone put their hands over my eyes. I could tell by the placement of calluses that it was Yves.

"Guess who?" he whispered. I played along, so as to keep his hands there a little longer.

"Sophia Loren?" I hazarded. He spun me around and hugged me.

"You little bitch, you knew it was me," he said.

"I was thrown by the strange smell on your hands."

"Pussy, little brother." He head-butted me affectionately. "Hey, did you get those leaky titty mags for me?"

"Yeah, they're in my bag," I said.

"Great. Hey, I want you to meet someone," he said as he pulled one of the neighbourhood girls into our sacred brotherly orbit.

"Buddy, this is Gloria. She's a dancer."

"I saw the Bolshoi Ballet in Montreal," I said.

"I table dance at Club Super Sexe," she replied. Yves, sensing the tension in the moment, jumped in.

"Buddy was the winner of the Prettiest Feet in All Quebec contest," he told her. "He spent the past year touring the province on a train."

"So what? I was the winner of the Best Breasts in All Quebec contest," she huffed, sticking her chest out. She had wet spots over the nipples.

"I see you've found the perfect woman," I said. He chose to ignore my crack. Gloria began rubbing her breasts against Yves, and everyone started talking about tractors. Apparently, Maman had recently bought a new one, and it was state-of-the-art. I suddenly felt an enormous distance, and so to bridge it, I started rubbing my breasts against Yves. I probably should have tried talking about tractors instead. He threw me off roughly and moved away. I went for the vodka.

The rest of the evening became a blur. It ended with everybody stripping naked and swimming out to L'Isles des Memoires. I got tired halfway because I had been smoking too much, so I stroked onto my back and lifted one leg out of the water like a dancer. I then dove under in one graceful movement and popped up in a different place, my arms waving like a cheerleader. It felt so great, I couldn't stop doing it. I noticed I had finally attracted the attention of my siblings.

"What are you doing?" asked Caresse.

"Water ballet," I responded. Everyone laughed and tried

copying my motions. We really got into it, and soon we had developed a routine. As the sun broke the darkness on Lac d'Eau, we had it down pat and performed an entire ballet from start to finish in perfect harmony, thereby inventing synchronized swimming.

Attawapiskat

In September, I went back to high school. My time in the sun had been exciting but now, just like Jodie Foster, it was time to leave stardom behind and return to the drab world of academia. It was hard. Everything in St. Hubert sur la Lac seemed stuck on pause, and everyone bored me silly. I wondered if my life had already peaked.

During my time away, a lot of things had changed. For one thing, a new school had been built and I was part of the very first class to grace its brand-new halls. Our little one-room schoolhouse had been turned into a Dairy Queen and now local yokels ate Brazier Burgers where Brother Aloysius once wielded his mighty strap. He came along to the new school even though it was no longer Catholic. He still taught in his robes, but everyone just thought he was a hippie. Since there was now a much larger student body, he could diversify and teach the subject he always loved the most—drama. I was the first to sign up. I thought it might lift me out of my doldrums.

One day, just after the new year began, we were in drama class. I had just smoked a joint with Maurice Legault out behind the school. He had a full beard by this time. The pot made me higher than I'd ever been. Brother Aloysius was droning on about the Meyerhold technique and I was fighting off waves of paranoia, so I decided to concentrate on something small. I began to watch the movement of Brother Aloysius's chalk as he wrote on the blackboard. I thought about how each stroke of the chalk imparted knowledge to us, all the while diminishing itself. This led me to muse on the very nature of existence and the cannibalizing effect of art and how we are all like chalk, scrawling our stories on the blackboard of being, until all that is left is the story. Suddenly, the chalk broke and stirred me from my reverie, and I realized that my story wasn't over. I still had a big piece of chalk. So I decided to write a play and cast everyone I knew. I would turn this sleepy little burg into a world-class theater destination, another Oberammergau. Or at least another Blyth.

My themes were grand, nothing less than life, death, the meaning of existence, and fashion. I called it *Attawapiskat*, an Indian word meaning . . . something or other. I never knew what, I just saw it on a map and said "Eureka!" I still don't know what "Eureka" means.

The play was nothing less than an overview of human history filled with real and fictional people. There were over 100 speaking parts, which means 101 speaking parts. Casting was daunting. I had to cast for roles as diverse as Tiberius, Tony the Tiger, Eve Arden, and Death. Most of my siblings scored choice parts, not because of nepotism, but because they were more willing to take their clothes off. In fact, all my brothers and sisters became involved in some way. Pascal did the lighting, Jeanne designed the costumes, Fleur kept everybody fed. I even had Guy pose bare-chested for the poster, but I wouldn't give him a part because he was so difficult to work with during that photo session. Claude and Jean-Claude built sets, and Davide wrote and performed the music on ukulele, bagpipes, and piano.

We rehearsed in the school auditorium every day after school for months, shaping and crafting the play beyond perfection. My sister Christianne, whom I had cast as the star of the show, was turning into a complete prima donna. Once, after throwing a cup of hot chocolate in her face, she stormed offstage in a hissy fit. She later apologized for provoking me. I had to forgive her. She just had too much damn talent.

Meanwhile, work progressed apace on the sets and costumes. Jeanne, working with no budget, turned old blankets into gowns, fishing lures into jewelry, and regular old moss into glorious, tumbling wigs. Because Claude and Jean-Claude were so inept, we went for a more minimalist approach to the sets. Pascal's lighting grids were nothing less than revolutionary, however. She actually punched holes in the roof of the auditorium, letting outdoor natural light and the indoor incandescence mingle together. At the tender age of thirty-two, you could just tell that girl was going places.

Even Maman got involved. I got her to play the role of Time, which entailed her sitting on an old kitchen chair at the side of the stage for the entire show. You're probably wondering how I convinced her to do it. It was simple. By this time in her life, she had become quite a drunk and her sight was going, so I just told her she was at home.

Everything was dovetailing perfectly. I felt like my life was finally making sense. There was to be one performance only, beginning at dawn and ending at sunset, with one brief intermission half an hour before the end of the play.

Act One had no human actors. The set was just a bare stage with tape recorders placed strategically about, playing actual family fights. Suspended over center stage was a cattle prod that swung to and fro over a large fruit basket. Two starving raccoons were released onstage, whereupon they would try to grab the food without getting shocked. Invariably the stunner would hit them and they would convulse and drop the fruit. It scandalized the good citizens of St. Hubert sur la Lac. Like Antonin Artaud's *Theater of Cruelty*, I wanted to wake them up out of their collective stupor. After a while the raccoons revolted and attacked the audience, much as I expected. They were immediately killed by sharpshooters and fashioned into hats for Act Three.

In Act Two we saw the introduction of actual human actors. The story went like this. Jesus (played by me) and the disciples are bored one day, so Jesus, who has just returned from a trip to the future, tells everyone about this marvelous new country he visited called Canada, and Matthew, always the drama queen, says, "Why not put on a play about the founding of Canada for Mary Magdalene and all her prostitute friends?" So they do, but then in the middle of the play they get so bored with the story of the founding of Canada they abandon the production and start whoring it up with Mary and her pals, which leads to an orgy. It climaxes with me as Jesus as Sir John A. MacDonald giving a half hour speech on the virtues of dullness. For my American readers, Sir John A. MacDonald was the first prime minister of Canada. He's sort of like our version of George Washington, and just like George, he had a terrible haircut, too.

In Act Three, the entire cast solemnly filed out naked, wearing nothing but raccoon hats from Act One and engaged in banter, just using slogans from television commercials. Pascal's lighting was foreboding and Germanic. Davide's score was sufficient, if you like that sort of thing. Personally, I would have written something a little more . . . musical. But that's just me, a perfectionist.

In Act Four, during a big production number predicting the rise of the charming serial killer in American film, someone noticed a horrible smell. After a thorough backstage search, we failed to find the culprit, and the play continued.

In Act Five, during a raunchy sex scene in a slag heap between Maurice Legault as a very dirty Pollution God and Caresse as Mother Nature, two people in the audience collapsed from the fumes. There was talk of closing the show down. Luckily, it was intermission. That's when Jean-Claude decided to search the stage. He found Maman dead in her chair, leaking a foul brown fluid.

"Let's work it into the show," I suggested desperately, sensing disaster.

"Buddy, it's Maman!" pleaded Caresse, crocodile tears pouring down her face.

"Maman would want us to finish the show," I told her. "She loved the theater. She lived for it. In fact, her last words to me were 'Lunt and Fontaine!' "

A figure stepped out from the cast. It was Christianne, dressed as the Virgin Mary. She looked bewitching. I rushed up to her.

"Christianne, your big scene is coming up next," I beseeched.

"Shut the fuck up. This show is over," she said. Someone brought the curtain down. There was nothing I could do.

I spent the next few days sniffing Plastic Wood in the attic and picking at a scab. When I finally went downstairs again, the funeral was over. No one had even missed me. It reminded me of the million other slights I had suffered during my time with this family. They didn't need me. They would never acknowledge my star quality. I no longer belonged. I had been a child for too many years. It was time to become a boy. So I decided to make my own way in the world. Late one night, while everyone slept, I crept downstairs, trying to keep my bulky suitcase from making noise. I remembered the sight of my brother Pierre doing the exact same thing years ago, and I thought to myself, Wow, this would be a great way to end this section of my autobiography.

A Place
to Stand,
a Place
to Grow

Well, that was quite a ride, wasn't it? I hope no one fell off. When I see it written down, my childhood seems positively Dickensian. And like all good Dickens heroes, I was now officially an orphan.

I had a vague plan to somehow make my way to Tokyo and become a rock star. I'd read somewhere that they really needed them, and I knew that I had what it took. Well, at least for Japan. If that didn't work out, I thought I might go to New York and become an avant-garde director in the new medium of video. I'd just label blank tapes with pretentious titles like "The Enigma Collision" and the resulting video would rocket me to stardom. And if that didn't work out, there was always the world famous Lloyd Bridges Oceanographic Institute in Bora Bora, where I was sure to be accepted as a student in the bold new field of interspecies communication as soon as they realized how well dolphins respond to a lisp.

I had so many aspirations, dear reader. I was so young and so cute. I just hoped I wouldn't end up hustling on the street, like *Alexander: The Other Side of Dawn*. But until my career got off the ground, I decided to go to Toronto and become a waiter.

Ontari-ari-ari-o!

Days later, I found myself hitchhiking alongside the Trans-Canada Highway. Eventually, a caramel Lincoln Town Car with a black leatherette roof pulled over and I got in. The driver was a little older than me, dark and handsome like Dean Martin, with slightly mad brown eyes. He wore a Calvin Klein T-shirt and designer jeans. I could tell he was gay. In fact, anyone could tell he was gay. I felt relief at knowing I wasn't the only queen in the world.

"Please don't slam the door," he said as I climbed in the front seat next to him, slamming the door behind me. He sighed deeply and affectedly.

"Buckle up!" he ordered as the car tore off, spitting gravel. I tried to chat but he would have none of it.

"Please don't speak," he snipped. "This is a difficult maneuver." The car swerved into the other lane, narrowly missing a green Dodge.

"Goddamn *Chinois!*" he screamed.

"Actually I don't think they were Chinese," I corrected.

"Well, they were both women, weren't they? Case closed." It turned out that he was going to Toronto, which fit with my plans. With a flourish, he pushed the cruise control button on the steering wheel and we settled back for the long trip.

"My name is Marco Nagy. It's Hungarian. Spelled N-A-G-Y but pronounced with a soft 'g' and a silent 'y.' I'm very particular about pronunciation," he said with a haughty air. He was hilarious. I sensed that we would become very good friends.

"My name's Buddy Cole."

"You look haunted, Buddy. Like you haven't used moisturizer in days." He looked at himself in the rearview mirror and smoothed his eyebrows.

"Due for a bit of hydrotherapy myself," he said quietly. He turned and looked at me for a long time. Long enough that he almost had another accident.

"Those damn Biafrans shouldn't be allowed to drive," he said, yanking the steering wheel savagely. "Too addled from famine." After he recovered from the near miss, he continued.

"What's your pH balance? You look slightly acidic to me," he said, sizing me up.

"More than slightly."

"I have some skin-care products in the backseat. Just grab that little black carryall," he said. I did so, and unzipped it. Inside were a multitude of products.

"See that little blue tube in there, with the adorable yellow top? That is aloe, the ultimate in restorative rejuvenation. Smell it." It smelled like nothing. "Isn't it incredible? You can smell the actual meadow from which it was harvested. Now, is there a little smoky rose quartz decanter?"

"Is this it?" I said, pulling out a little smoky rose quartz decanter.

"No, the other one." Sure enough, there was another little smoky rose quartz decanter, this one a bit bigger.

"Remove the lid, place the baby finger flush to the top, then turn it over gently. Don't shake or you'll disturb the essential oils. Now release the finger and apply the tiniest dollop of elixir under the eye area. Just pat, don't rub. How does that feel?"

"Tingly."

"Now, look in the mirror, and compare." I did so. Both sides looked exactly the same, except one side was wet.

"It really works," I said sarcastically.

"You laugh now, but you'll see. In a few years, when the signs of age begin to creep through the cracks of your skin and marginalize your beauty to the edges of acceptability, then we'll see who's laughing." He wrenched at the wheel again.

"Goddamn Turks!" he yelled, narrowly missing another vehicle. "What is this? Turkish surprise?" For the first time in my life, I felt like I was along on someone else's ride, a burr caught in a pimp's fox fur coat. This wasn't my style, but the way I felt after all that had happened, I'd have gotten in a car with Wayne Gacy.

"Where are you from, Buddy?" he asked.

"St. Hubert sur la Lac."

"That sounds like the nothing nowhere-*ville* of all time. I myself am from Ottawa, the nation's capital. I'm going to be a model, Buddy. You've got the look, too. Why don't you toss in your lot with me?"

"I don't know. I really want to act and dance," I said.

"Dance? Are you insane? No offense, but dance is on its last legs. Vaudeville is more vital. Well, nature calls. Let's pull over into that hideous roadside establishment and drain our boyish bladders."

We parked and hopped out. Marco said he wanted to buy some gum first, so I went ahead to the bathroom. There were eight cubicles and several men skulking about washing their hands at the sink and combing their hair. I went into one, pushed my pedal pushers down, and sat down on the commode. I noticed a hole in the wall next to the toilet paper dispenser, and I thought, Oh, how clever. If you run out of toilet paper, you can reach in and get some from the other stall.

I amused myself reading the graffiti. It appeared that a lot of men wanted to give or get blow jobs. Suddenly, an erect cock came through the hole. So I followed the directions on the wall. When it was over, whoever it was quickly ran out the door, and I tidied myself up, hoping Marco had not left. He hadn't.

"Well, we're off," Marco said, as the Lincoln Town Car veered gaily into traffic. After settling into his lane, he began to speak.

"I had a little episode," he confided.

"What do you mean?" I asked.

"Well, you got it out of me. Someone blew me in the washroom through a glory hole. I'm surprised you didn't hear me."

"Can I have a piece of gum?" I asked him abruptly. He pulled out some Dentyne.

"Recommended by four out of five dentists," he said, twirling the wheel. The car fell into silence as we listened to the radio, and I vowed to never again use a glory hole. It got dark and we decided to spend the night in a fleabag roadside motel.

"Well it's a total miserable-o-rama," said Marco, tossing down the carryall as we walked into the dank room. "We better make ourselves uncomfortable." There was only one bed. We both looked at it.

"Look," said Marco, turning to me. "I just want you to know that even though you are a very attractive youth like myself, and that nature seems to cry out for our union, I just have to say that you're not my type, and I will not be available for intercourse. No hard feelings. I'm sure we will become very good friends, but there will be no hanky-panky."

"That's fine. I feel the exact same way."

"Understood."

"I'm exhausted," I said. "I'm ready for bed."

"Me, too," said Marco. "Do you need the washroom, because I need to wash my face."

"I can wait," I said. Two hours later, I was still waiting. I banged on the door.

"I'll be a minute," came the reply. The shower had been running the whole time, so the room was filled with steam. Finally, he emerged. It looked like he had taken a sander to his face.

"Well, what do you think? Dewy youth?"

"You have the skin texture of a fetus," I said. He dug into the carryall, pulled out an eye visor, and put it on.

"Let's get some beauty sleep," he said, and lay down flat on his back with his arms by his sides, immediately unconscious. I washed up in the bathroom and then lay down in the bed next to him, drifting off to sleep.

The story of b

The drive to Toronto was uneventful, save for Marco's endless barrage of ethnic slurs, which continued to increase in absurdity until he was eventually attacking even the Walloons of Belgium. Although on that one, I had to agree. We arrived late in the day and checked into a gay guest house called The Saunter On Inn. A scary leatherman with a droopy mustache, dark pouchy eyes, and nipples the size of gooseberries was at the reception desk. His name was Uli.

"So, you boys fuck each other?" he asked out of the blue.

"None of your business, leather freak," blasted back Marco.

"Is there a minibar in the room?" I asked, interjecting a note of humanity.

"No, but there is a dungeon, and there's a bar in the lounge. Happy Hour starts in a half an hour."

"I think we've heard enough," sneered Marco. "Don't bother to carry our bags. You seem to have enough of your own." And with that we whirled away. The room was another dump. We unpacked our clothes and got dressed.

"What do you think?" I asked as I spun around the room in my outfit—a pair of very slutty white jeans shorts, a red plaid shirt cinched at the waist, and cowboy boots sprayed silver. I had also managed to blow-dry my long blond hair into the shape of a cowboy hat. Marco took me in with a glance.

"I can't say I agree with all your choices," he admitted.

"You're being diplomatic."

"What can I say? I'm from Ottawa," he responded. "Now, let's get happy."

Downstairs, a tawdry scene was unraveling. There was a gaggle of fags (also known as a "faggle") talking about Susan Lucci being robbed of an Emmy, a discussion that continues to this very day. We got our drinks and then took a seat as far away from the others as possible.

"Buddy, first thing tomorrow morning, we go to a talent agency and announce to the peon at the reception desk that we are here and we are ready to be photographed for magazines and television and beyond," said Marco.

"And that we're also ready for major roles in feature films," I added. "I wonder what my first role will be? An action picture, a romantic comedy, a film noir? Or maybe one of those films that comes around once in a generation that changes all the rules."

"That's the beauty of what your beauty will do for you," said Marco. He flagged down Uli.

"Barkeep? Two more!" Marco called out lustily.

"Actually, I was already bringing you two drinks. They're from that man over there," said Uli, pointing to a figure in the corner that neither of us had noticed before. He was a light-skinned black man, with long curly hair in a ponytail and a thin mustache. He was wearing an expensive cream silk shirt that was wide open, exposing a chest covered with corkscrew curls and lots of gold jewelry. I thought he was sexy, but Marco thought he looked evil, which was my point exactly.

"He's coming over," I exclaimed. We watched as the man slid across the room and into the empty seat next to me.

"*Je suis Natas,*" he said. "*J'aime beaucoup tes cheveux.*"

"*Merci bien. Mon nom est Buddy,*" I responded. "How did you know I understand French?"

"I know all about you," he whispered in my ear. I pulled away for the sake of the children.

"Natas, this is my friend Marco."

"Howdoyoudo," said Marco in one dismissive slur.

"That's an interesting accent you have, Natas. What is that?" I asked.

"Haitian," he said.

"Where's Haitia?" asked Marco.

"In the West Indies. And Marco, it's Haiti," I said, stressing every syllable.

"Perfect wording," said Marco, looking elsewhere.

"I live near here. Why don't we all go back to my place for a little party?" said Natas, gripping my knee under the table. I thought about Papa's advice, and how stupid it was.

"Count me out," said Marco. "I have a busy day tomorrow fielding offers. So do you, Buddy." He looked at me with concern.

"I'll be fine." I shrugged off his gambit.

"Okay. Then, I'll be off. Nice meeting you, Nada. Take good care of my friend Buddy. He's a prize." He left. Natas's hand was now on my thigh.

"Let's go," I said. "Happy Hour is almost over."

"On the contrary, it has just begun," Natas growled. When we got to his pitch-black Jaguar with a red leather interior, he stopped me gently and asked me to wear a silk scarf, which I tied around my neck insouciantly.

"No, it goes around your eyes," he corrected.

"But then I wouldn't be able to see."

"Exactly. That way, you have to depend on your other senses even more, thereby awakening them. By the time we get to the apartment, your entire body will have become your eyes."

"That sounds exciting," I said. I wasn't so sure, but I did it anyway. The worst he could do was kill me.

We rode for what seemed like hours, Natas stroking my leg and whispering dirty things in my ear the entire time. I was woozy with excitement. Finally we stopped. I heard Natas get out, walk around the car, and open my door. The click of his boots on the pavement was like the sound of castanets inside my head.

We walked into what seemed like an apartment lobby. I knew this because we passed someone who was saying, "This is a beautiful apartment lobby." We got into an elevator and went up many floors. The doors opened and we walked down the hall and into an apartment. The blindfold was removed. I blinked in the light. Before me was a vision of pure horror—a large, framed print of a ballerina's feet.

"Do you like my picture?" he asked.

"Yes, and I'm so glad my senses are heightened for it."

He disappeared into the kitchen. I looked around the room. Nothing special, just some nondescript furniture, the odd pair of shoes, clothes scattered about, and a human skull on a glass coffeetable. Natas reentered the room, carrying two vodka martinis. I took a sip.

"It tastes odd."

"I put in a bit of Haitian tincture, to heighten the vodka."

"It seems everything is about heightening with you. What's your feeling about hemlines this season? Am I talking loudly? Did I just say what I thought I said? Is my mouth melting?" The room swam in front of my eyes. I thought I was going to faint. I looked at Natas. He was sitting straight as an arrow, staring at me.

"You drugged me," I said. "Do I owe you?"

"*Vous êtes mortes,*" he replied, menacingly.

That's funny, I thought, switching to the formal *vous* like that. Not very friendly. And what does he mean by "dead"?

That was my last coherent thought until I woke up in a luxurious bed, with Marco standing over me, holding a martini.

"Where am I?" I muttered, my voice cracking like a dehydrated octogenarian.

"Buddy! You're alive! Sweet mother of the holy brat, this is a day of celebration."

"The last thing I remember was having a drink at Natas's place." I could hardly talk.

"That was almost a year ago."

"What?" I croaked, trying to sit up but unable to move. Then Marco filled me in on what had transpired during my lost year, and what a tale it was. Apparently, that night Natas had drugged me with a voodoo potion and turned me into a zombie. Then he had put me to work in his Haitian restaurant, Voodoo Chile, as a zombie busboy.

The entire staff were zombies who were kept in a shed in the back. Natas was the maître d'. Patrons thought that the whole thing was a put-on and that the zombies were just actors. Sort of like those theme restaurants, where people pretend to be at a medieval feast. The only other nonzombie was the cook, a tiny malevolent bushman from Johannesburg named Xingu. He was a big coke addict who couldn't keep a job. This was his seventeenth restaurant. His specialties were curried dog, hummingbird heart tarte, and his masterpiece, shredded cardboard salad, inspired by the cardboard shantytowns of Port-au-Prince. It was served with a vinaigrette made from barrel rainwater and fetid hoof. The cardboard salad was a huge hit because it had zero calories and caused diarrhea. It was therefore a favorite of fashion models. Luckily, the restaurant had seven washrooms.

According to Marco, I laboured there for almost a year, clearing tables and reciting the dessert menu in the calm, measured tones of the undead. Then one fateful day Marco came into Voodoo Chile with his new best friend, a fat, bubbly, blond woman named Carma Norma. Carma was independently wealthy, having invented the Carma Norma Bum Pads for Men, a little augmentation for those not gifted in the seat. Rich as she was, though, she always looked like a slob in public, favouring shapeless circus-tent clothing.

The two of them were both celebrating. Marco had just signed a lucrative contract as the face of La Ricotta Facial Mud Masque for Men. He was going to be the first male supermodel. We're still waiting. And Carma was turning forty. Their waiter that night was Zombie Blair. He wore a name tag that said HI, MY NAME WAS BLAIR. He was very handsome, even with his yellow eyes and blue-gray skin. I think I fucked him once, but I can't be sure.

"I just love how the waiters act like zombies, isn't that great?" shrieked Carma. "We should do this all the time, go around talking like that. Wouldn't that be fun? Let's do it, Marco! Ahhhhh!" she screamed with glee.

"Carma, calma," said Marco. "You're forty now. Act like an adult." Marco snapped his fingers and called for the busboy. I staggered over.

"Look, busboy. I'm sure you're all very proud of both your food and your performances as zombies. Both are excellent. But I'm interested only in the check."

According to Marco, he hadn't recognized me yet because of the dark circles under my eyes and my waxen pallor. But the moment I spoke, the jig was up.

"I'll-get-your-check-immediately-sir," I robotically lisped.

"Buddy! Good lord, it's you!" he screamed, embracing me. "You have a job. That's good. I'm the new face of La Ricotta Facial Mud Masque for Men and you're starring as a zombie busboy. Success all around. Of course, I'm mad at you for running off that night, but that's in the past. Come, meet my friend Carma Norma."

"Thank-you-for-coming-to-Voodoo-Chile," I continued.

"So in character, I love it. Now snap out of it. I haven't seen you in a year. It's me, Marco. Remember?" I just stared. At that moment, Natas noticed the disturbance and came over.

"Excuse me, sir, does there seem to be a problem?" he asked. Marco recognized him instantly and put two and three together.

"Five! You're that goddamn geisha from Haitia we met a year ago. That was the same night Buddy disappeared. Wait a minute, there's a connection here, and I'm going to find it. I've found it! That didn't take long at all. My mind is working at top speed. You kidnapped Buddy Cole and turned him into a zombie."

"Did you get the check yet?" said Carma Norma, despair etched into her forty-year-old face.

"I'm calling the police," said Marco.

"But don't you have coke on you?" asked Carma Norma, panic leaking through her oversized pores.

"Just residue on my credit cards. I'll lick them before the cops come," he answered. "After all, this is my best friend Buddy."

"But I'm your best friend," pleaded Carma Norma.

"Shut up! I can't think!" Marco shouted.

"What do you want?" asked Natas coldly.

"I promise not to call the police if you release my friend from your voodoo clutches, and, as a goodwill gesture, tear up the check."

Natas agreed. And with that, Marco and Carma spirited me off to his apartment, where, through intense massage and liberal doses of chilled vodka administered intravenously, I finally emerged from my zombie coma.

Millennium

The next few months were taken up with recuperation, rehabilitation, and rejuvenation. Soon I was as fresh as the dew on a virgin's mons, and was zooming around Marco's apartment in an electric wheelchair. But then one day, Marco came home, after a hard day of looking gorgeous.

"Buddy, you've been here for months now, and we've been getting along famously, but I think it's time you got the fuck out of that wheelchair," he said, pushing me onto the floor. I was startled.

"I'm sorry for the rude behaviour, but when I see you wallowing in self-pity like an aging actress, it moves me to action, and that's why I kicked you onto the floor. Out of love. Now get up and walk. Don't lie there like a bag of old Miami Jew balls."

What could I say to that? He was right. It was time to move on. Whatever had happened to me during my year as a zombie was in the past. I moved back in to The Saunter On Inn. Uli let me stay there for free, as he felt guilty for introducing me to Natas. I slept on a sling in the dungeon. I was so exhausted from pounding the pavement looking for work all day that I barely noticed the leathermen bustling about at night. Once the last diehard had staggered out, Uli would come in and tenderly toss an old flannel blanket over me.

Every day, I would get dressed up in my "looking for work" outfit—black tights, Chinese slippers, an oversized white men's shirt belted at the waist, and a beret worn off to one side. Then one day I saw a sandwich board on the sidewalk on Yonge Street for an agency called MegaStar Talent Agency, requesting "Leading Men for Movies and TV!" I followed the arrow that led to a back alley that led to a rusty door that led to a long, narrow staircase that led to a padlocked door. On the door was a sign written on the back of a scrap of paper, stating that MegaStar Talent had moved to a new location on Eastern Avenue.

So there I went. The address was a little house, a sad slice of toast in an industrial part of the city where only cruising homosexuals and gay bashers roamed. Nature at work. I looked through the screen door into a dark cluttered living room. I knocked.

"Door's open," came the response. I walked in. There was a shapeless shape in the darkness sitting on a couch covered by a Phentex quilt.

"I came about your sandwich board," I said.

"Oh, good. Bring it here," she said. I didn't understand.

"Pardon me?"

"Oh, you're not the sandwich boy. Fuck, I'm going to starve. Okay. What's your name?"

"Buddy Cole," I replied. "I want to be an actor."

"Good. Now, Buddy, the first thing we need are eight-by-tens. We need a résumé. And get some clothes! Honey, you'll be auditioning for *male* roles."

And that was my introduction to my agent Doris Coon-come Fahrazi Dimvale Davis Hurtubrise. She had kept each of her husband's names, but when I knew her she was between spouses.

She did all of her business in an incredibly cluttered front room, sitting on a broken-down chesterfield, clutching a rye and ginger ale and smoking roll-your-owns. Everywhere on the wall were pictures of her actor clients, all mingled up with photos of her four ex-husbands. She had dyed jet-black hair that fell in a thick, unkempt braid down her back, and she always wore tight black sweaters and black slacks. They were always covered in cat hair, although in all the years I knew her I never saw a cat.

The first thing I did was have my pictures done. I brought the contact sheets to Doris. She looked through the pictures of me swimming, riding a horse, playing backgammon, firing a gun, and making faces while wearing wigs, but finally chose a simple shot of me feeding a goldfish.

I would go in every couple of days to see if there were any auditions, and she would sit really close to me on the couch and rub against me. I would become very dignified, like Deborah Kerr trying to ignore a dog humping her leg at a classy function, and she would eventually get the hint and stop. At the time I was disgusted, but now, after hundreds of drunken come-ons of my own, I'm more understanding.

Months flew by, but no matter what I did Doris never seemed to send me on any auditions. Then one day I decided to take the bull by the horns.

"Doris, I really think it's time I went out on an audition."

"Yes, we must get you out there."

"Good. So, when?"

"Well, first of all, we have to let people know what you can do. Show them that Buddy Cole is versatile, that he can play anything from the guy on the street to the guy behind the counter."

"Exactly. I think we're both on the same wavelength here. So, when?"

"You're like a Ryan O'Neal or a Jeff Bridges waiting to happen."

"That may be, but when?" She put her hand on my knee.

"It's all there. It just needs to be brought out. I'm going to help you with that. You have a wonderful body. That's very important for an actor. It's his tool. It's how we actors tell our stories."

"I didn't know you were an actor," I said.

"Oh, yeah. For years. I was good. No, I was great. Gorgeous, too. I had long black hair. Thin little Barbie waist. Don't laugh, I was thin. I looked like friggin' Cher. Now all I have is big tits. Feel them."

"I should go."

"Before you do, I saw something today in the breakdowns that might be right for you."

"What is it?"

"It's the role of the Time Gate Operator in a new American science fiction film called *Millennium*. It's about a government agent from the future who accidentally leaves a laser gun back in the past, which causes a ripple in the fabric of time called a temporal anomaly."

"Sounds stupid," I exclaimed. "When's the audition?"

"Whenever you *really* want it," she purred. "You've got great gams."

"I walk a lot," I replied.

"It shows." Her hand went to my thigh.

"Who's in the movie?" I asked.

"Kris Kristofferson and Cheryl Ladd." Cheryl Ladd? She was an Angel. This sounded big. Doris's breasts pressed into my shoulder.

"How many lines?"

"Two, but you say them directly to Cheryl," she said, her hand squeezing my basket. That was all I needed to hear. It was that, or work my way up slowly. In other words, theater. I'd rather die. The actual details of the tryst are unimportant. Let's just say that it was something you'd only see on the Discovery Channel. Later, I auditioned and got the part. I was on my way.

On my first day on the set, one of the suits from L.A. informed me that I would have to shave my head, as I was playing a character far in the future where everyone had cancer and had gone bald. I suddenly noticed that all the extras in the room were bald. I informed the suit from L.A. that the only reason to shave one's head was for lice, and since that obviously wasn't the case with me, there would be no need. At that point, a muscular skinhead extra named Mike announced that if I wouldn't do the role, he would.

"No one's talking to you!" I plunged in foolhardily. He immediately came up beside me and put his ugly mug close to my face. He hissed in my ear that I had better watch myself, because the moment he got me alone, I was dead. The suit from L.A. ignored the threat, as he was going through my hair with a comb. Suddenly he shrieked and held up his hand. Crushed between the nails of his thumb and pointing finger was a tiny, struggling figure.

"Ah-ha! Lice!" he screamed.

"Let me see that," I demanded. He extended his fingers, pinching the offending creature. I looked closely.

"Wait a minute. That's a crab," I corrected. Ten minutes later I was as bald as an old tire. And ten minutes after that, they shaved my head. And ten minutes after that, I was being fitted with a huge headpiece that completely obscured my scalp. Ah, well, I thought. That's Hollywood North.

Because both of my lines were to Miss Cheryl Ladd, I knew I had to be good. For five days I acted opposite Miss Ladd and she never once spoke to me or even looked over. She just stared straight ahead into that actor's middle distance where Oscar dwells. Kris was all grizzled handsomeness and "acting's for fags" stoicism. He also just stared straight ahead. I imagined him writing a song in his mind about fucking Cheryl or decking her, or else fucking her on his deck.

As the shoot went on, Mike the skinhead continued his reign of terror. Whenever I looked his way, he would make a motion of slitting my throat. I decided to stick to the open areas as much as I could, which was difficult as the set was a massive time machine and government complex in an old, abandoned factory. There were lots of places in which to get lost.

The extras' holding pen was a mini former Yugoslavia, consisting of white supremacist skinheads and nonracist skinheads of all colours, so fights often broke out. Oddly enough, Mike was in the nonracist group, but that didn't mean he couldn't hate fags. I told the suit from L.A. of my precarious situation but he just shrugged and said that if I got hurt, I would receive compensation, but that if I got killed, I would be replaced.

Mike became increasingly threatening, so I decided to make some friends in the opposing camp for protection. I befriended a young Nazi named Flea 45. One day we were in a part of the set that wasn't being used, on a fifteen-minute break. All around us loomed giant glass cylinders filled with some sort of yellow fluid. Suspended inside were heads with a million wires coming out of their necks. The idea was that these were the leaders of the future whose bodies had been eaten away by cancer. They looked like people pickles.

I was smoking a cigarette when Flea 45 squatted down on the floor and brought something out of his pocket. It was a short length of rubber hose. He looped it around his arm and then tied it tight. His veins bulged. Then, all the time staring straight at me, he took out a little packet of brown powder and poured it into a bent spoon that had just appeared. He lit a lighter under it and turned it into a liquid. He then took out a needle, sucked up all the fluid, and plunged it home. Ah-ha, I thought. A diabetic. He slumped back against one of the glass cylinders and his eyes closed. The heads of future cancer-ridden leaders bobbed in the yellow brine behind him. I stared at Flea 45's beautiful, tough face and thought about kissing him, but before I had the chance, his eyes fluttered open and he finally spoke.

"Wanna shoot up?"

"No, thanks," I said. "I'm too afraid of spoons."

Then came my last day, the day we were to film the climactic Time Quake. Let me explain. The temporal anomaly, which I mentioned before, was now moving toward the future, or our present, and when it hit, a Time Quake would destroy everything! I told you it was stupid.

I was nervous because this was Mike's last chance to get me. The shot was a very complicated one, with dozens of extras and pyrotechnics. I felt he might take advantage of the confusion to make his move. Finally, everything was set. It was just me and Cheryl and a hundred warring skinheads. Something for everyone. The director called "Action!" and Cheryl turned to address me. I was wrong. She could move her head.

"What's happening, Time Gate Operator?"

"Time Quake!" I shrieked. "Time Quake!"

There was a massive *BOOM!* right behind me. I began to run in the direction I'd been told. More explosions went off, one close to my head. All around me was pandemonium. Skinheads rushed roughly by like rapids. Suddenly Mike was at my side. Something shiny flashed in his hand. It was a knife. He lunged. I was going to be stabbed. Then, out of nowhere, a hand holding a bent spoon deflected the blow. It was Flea 45. He brought his arm back and then somehow plunged the spoon deep into Mike's gut. Mike went down. Flea 45 grabbed my arm and we fled. My racist hero.

Mike survived. In fact he got a lot of money by suing the movie company, saying that he had been hit by shrapnel. So everybody was happy. It was time for me and Flea 45 to say good-bye.

"Will I ever see you again?" I asked him, leaning seductively against the craft service table.

"I'm in the phone book," he said, drifting off into the non-union special business extra night.

Later, when the movie came out, I brought Marco, Carma,

and Doris to the premiere. When my big moment arrived, I discovered that my voice had been dubbed, making me sound like James Earl Jones. I guess there's no sibilance in the future.

"Don't worry, honey," said Doris, putting a positive spin on the whole affair. "There will be lots of roles. And in some of them, you'll be able to use your own voice."

"You're such a dreamer," I replied. I turned to Marco. "What did you think of me in the movie?"

"You were in it? Ah, so that's why we came. You were wonderful, then."

Doris was wrong. I never actually did appear on film again, unless you count the footage of me standing in front of that tank in Tiananmen Square.

A tonic for the age

One day, after another particularly humiliating audition experience, I went home to my new basement apartment. I was subletting from a clown who was on tour, so the place was filled with masks, red noses, and big shoes hanging on the wall. There was only one advantage. I got to use his unicycle.

I made myself a martini and plopped down in front of the little black and white television for an evening of utter sloth. Everything was shit until I finally came across a talk show with a tawdry set, dim lighting, and idiotic people babbling about gardening. I watched, rivetted. When it was over, the credits said that it had been produced by Rogers Community Cable, a new cable facility dedicated to the interests of the community. A phone number flashed at the bottom of the screen. I jotted it down and made the call that would change my life. I was given an appointment the next morning at ten o'clock.

The studio was tiny, and situated in an abandoned strip mall near the Toronto Abbatoir, but the antenna was large and impressive. I poked my head in and seeing only a sleeping security guard, I went inside. I heard noise coming from behind a heavy door labeled ON THE AIR. DO NOT ENTER. I opened it and entered. A group of smokers were kneeling around card tables playing Bingo, while a gospel choir sang out the numbers in thundering tones. The cameraman, a balding, burly guy with a thick mustache, came over to me. He spoke in hushed tones.

"May I help you?"

"Shouldn't you be filming it?" I pointed toward his camera, which had drifted down and was aiming at the floor.

"Believe me, no one's watching the Evangelical Bingo Hour."

"Maybe they would if it was just a half hour."

"That's a great idea." He checked his watch and switched off the camera. "Who are you, anyway?"

"My name's Buddy Cole. I have an appointment."

"Oh, yes, Mr. Cole. My name's Philip Sheffield. I'm the station manager, floor director, cameraman, chief cook and bottle washer. The only thing I don't do is windows," he said, laughing at his own joke. I liked him instantly. I like people who think they're funny even when they aren't.

Mr. Sheffield's office was tiny and incredibly bare. He sat down behind his desk, on which was a fountain pen, a notepad, an ashtray, and a picture of the Queen visiting the cable station during one of her many royal visits.

"Ah, I see you noticed my picture. That was my proudest moment, when a Queen Elizabeth impersonator visited the station. So, what's the idea for your show? Hit me."

"It's not exactly a show, Mr. Sheffield. More a tonic for the age. Have you been getting the same feeling that I've been getting recently, that there's been something missing in television programming, but you don't know what it is? Like before, when there was just black and white and no one could imagine colour TV. Now we take colour for granted. We'd kill the person who would take away our colour. This is what I'm talking about, sir. Colour."

"So you do a painting show?" he asked.

"In a way. I paint with people."

"Will there be girls?"

"In a manner of speaking. There will be a girl doll, and her name is Cornygirl, and she has so much personality for a corn cob, it's unbelievable. In fact, she has more life than most of my friends. Not that any of the dull ones will be on the show. I see the possibility of doing remotes, possibly in South America, maybe the Middle East, wherever the killing fields are. Straight-up investigative reporting. I see a lot of celebrities on the show. I know I can get Cheryl Ladd and Kris Kristofferson."

"Okay. You've got the show."

"What? That's it?"

"Sure. I'd give you a show if all you wanted to do was stand there and piss on yourself. You've got the Thursday eight to eight thirty p.m. time slot."

"Oh. Prime time. Thank you. We'll see you on Thursday night, then."

I was very excited, and now I had to figure out what I was going to do. From what I could gather, television was just a bunch of amazing outfits, some chairs, a topic, guests, and a backdrop. Well, the outfits were easy. I decided on polka dots, which I figured could also be a topic. That was two down. For guests, I'd get Marco and Carma Norma. The backdrop, I'd paint myself. I decided on a large pair of red lips. But I still needed chairs. The only furniture I owned was a lawn chair, and my old wheelchair. I needed one more. Luckily Marco came to the rescue and bought me a four-hundred-dollar chair as a gift. It looked like a normal kitchen chair but according to Marco it was fabulous because it cost four hundred dollars. I was set.

Now all I needed was a title. Something that would draw them in, something bold and original. I had it! *M*A*S*H*. After all, it had worked once before, and that was a horrible show.

Finally it was zero hour. Thursday, 8:00 p.m. I took my

place on set, in the wheelchair, placed Cornygirl on the four-hundred-dollar chair, and waited nervously as the theme song played. I wrote the theme song myself. It went like this:

M*A*S*H,
This show isn't
M*A*S*H,
Yet it is a smash!
So sit back and enjoy
Buddy and his toy
Cornygirl Cornygirl Cornygirl Cornygirl!

The red light above camera one clicked on, and I felt light on my face. I boldly looked right into the lens and began.

"Hello, and welcome to *M*A*S*H*, the show that isn't set in Korea and doesn't star any of your favourite characters from *M*A*S*H* but does have a pair of hot lips," I said, motioning to my backdrop.

"So, now that you're hooked, let me introduce myself. My name is Buddy Cole, and I'm . . . well, I'm not exactly your host. I'm actually the host's best friend. Or more precisely, hostess. She's very shy, and has asked me to be her mouth-piece, which I have humbly accepted. Her name is Cornygirl."

Mr. Sheffield zoomed in on Cornygirl, who was wearing a polka-dot dress. Her clip-on mike looked adorable.

"Isn't she great? We've known each other since we were little. She's very jealous. She won't even let me have a dog. As you can see, both Cornygirl and I are wearing polka dots today, which also happens to be the topic of the show. My guest is the woman who created the Carma Norma Bum Pad for Men, Ms. Carma Norma herself. And with her is her walker, top model Mr. Marco Nagy. Welcome."

Marco came out stage left and Carma Norma came out stage right, so Mr. Sheffield split the difference and zoomed in on my feet. Marco sat in the lawn chair, and Carma Norma plopped herself down on the four-hundred-dollar chair, her full weight coming down on poor Cornygirl. I realized I was one chair short. I held my tongue. Cornygirl was a tough little cob, and the show must go on.

"Hello, Buddy," said Marco. "I hear your topic is polka dots. Well, the only one whoever poked Dot was Little Lotta. Speaking of which, Carma Norma! Are you enjoying the four-hundred-dollar chair?"

"It feels like my spine is finally being listened to," she replied, making herself comfortable.

"Carma, what about the issue of men and polka dots. Is it appropriate, or is it even legal?" I asked.

"As you know, I created the Carma Norma Bum Pad for Men, and naturally, therefore, I feel that polka dots are fine for a man."

"Do you have anything to drink, Buddy?" asked Marco. "Is all television such a desert? I'm sure I've seen pictures of Rhoda with a soda."

"There's tap water in the bathroom."

"Well, that won't do! Buddy, I can't continue. I must leave the set in search of beverage!" He got up and did so. There was a silence.

"Carma Norma, you're sitting on Cornygirl," I said. "Normally I wouldn't say anything, but she is the hostess of the show. And you and I have never been alone before. And frankly, I'm discovering that we have nothing to talk about. I'm exquisitely uncomfortable right now. How about you?"

"I have to get up?"

"Yes, just move over to Marco's chair," I suggested.

She looked at the flimsy lawn chair with the fear that only the very fat know. So, thinking quickly, she decided to bail, and ran off the set without a word. Luckily, Cornygirl was unharmed. Just very warm. I stared at the camera. I didn't know what to do. I had to give my audience something.

Then I had an idea. I sucked in my cheeks and started

holding my face in different ways—looking up from downward eyes, pursing my lips and raising one eyebrow. Then I started to frame my face with my hands in dramatic poses in an effort to project movie-star glamour. Then, moved by sheer panic, I got up and began to dance like a model, my hands whirling about my face and body, thereby inventing "vogueing." This went on for the rest of the show until I collapsed onto the four-hundred-dollar chair, looking like a ten-dollar whore. I realized I was sitting on Cornygirl, but was too tired to move. That's when Marco chose to return from his beverage search, holding a can of fruit juice.

"I'm back. Kudos to you, Buddy, you were marvelous. We were watching it at the convenience store on the surveillance camera. Where's Carma Norma?"

"She left."

"There goes my ride! By the way, what was the consensus on polka dots? I must know."

"The rules keep changing."

"Don't they, though."

"Well, that's all the time we have for tonight," I said to the camera. "Join us next week when Cornygirl and I welcome Cheryl Ladd and Kris Kristofferson. Good night."

"Cut!" came Mr. Sheffield's voice. "Great show, Buddy."

"Really?"

"Well, you didn't piss yourself. See you next week," he said, leaving.

"I guess they'll air any old shit," said Marco.

"Lucky for us."

Schwab's

Around this time my financial situation became dire. *Millennium* had been my only acting job for years and *M*A*S*H* had cost more than it made, so I was forced to get a real job. That was not an option, so I took up the position as Marco's personal assistant. His career as a top model was soaring, in a low altitude male model sort of way, so he could sort of afford to have a friend around to humiliate in exchange for a sort of a salary.

One day, we were on our way to a modeling assignment for Juicy Mango Jeans when he transformed from friend to boss before my very eyes. It was an ugly morphing, like Michael Jackson smashing up that car and turning into a panther in *Black or White*. Not for children.

"You will make sure that when I go to the set, that I am lint-free, that my carriage is regal, and that my concentration is absolute. I want no insolence. This will be difficult for you with your raging ego, but I know how much you need the money." I said nothing.

We drove through the gates of the studio. The security guard leaned into our window. Marco's passions were running high.

"Name, please?"

"Marco Nagy. I'm on the list." The guard checked his notes.

"I'm sorry, I can't find your name."

"It's spelled N-A-G-Y."

"I'm sorry, no. You're going to have to leave. Please back up out of the parking lot," he said. Marco pounced.

"Listen, you sleazy employee-of-the-month. I'm Marco Nagy, top model of this whole goddamn studio. Without me, you wouldn't even draw a salary. They'd pay you in salt, like a Roman centurion." Sensing blood, I immediately went into assistant mode.

"Excuse me, Officer? Is this not a photography studio where models come to be photographed?"

"Yes, it is, sir."

"Look at this face," I said, motioning toward Marco's scowling visage. "Is this not the face of a top model?" The man looked closely at Marco and hesitated.

"Well, then, what about me? Don't I look like the companion to a world-class model?" He had to agree and waved us in. Marco was a little peeved at my brio but he said nothing. We finally got to the hair and makeup room. Makeup and Hair were two beautiful women, one a blonde and one a redhead. The blonde introduced herself as Laughter, and the redhead said her name was Cunt. She explained that she had taken that name for political reasons, that she was reclaiming the word.

Marco was eager to begin and plopped himself down into the makeup chair so they could work their magic. Then he immediately sent me off to fetch a beverage, fruit juice of some kind, but not orange, grapefruit, mango, cherry, or apple. Luckily, the craft service table had plenty of pomegranate juice.

I ran back with my booty. Laughter and Cunt were putting the finishing touches on Marco. He looked ghastly, but I knew that honesty is the worst policy in the fashion world. I told him he looked younger than the day he was born. Then the wardrobe mistress came in carrying an outfit. Her name was Mary Woodrow. She handed him a pair of jeans and a T-shirt. Then Marco insisted we all leave the room so he could change into his outfit. How odd, I thought. I'd never known him to be so modest. We all filed out.

Minutes later, Marco came out of the room and posed. The jeans really worked. His ass looked like a ripe mango ready to fall out of a tree. Ahhh, I thought. If only asses fell out of trees, I'd be in the woods all the time.

"Well?" he asked. We all clapped sycophantically and followed him out to the set.

"Which one's the photographer?" he said, casting about for someone in authority. A snarky older woman with salt-and-pepper hair came striding over.

"I'm the photographer. Are you the model?" she said in a New York accent.

"I most certainly am," he grandly replied.

"Okay, stand over there," she ordered.

"Excuse me, I'm not used to working this way. I'm accustomed to working *with* the photographer, not being ordered around like a circus animal."

"Okay, right, here's the shot. You stand in front of the lights, and I take a picture. Got it?" she said. I leaned in and whispered to Marco, who was on the verge of saying something he might regret for the rest of his life.

"I know I'm just your assistant, but try to refrain from calling her a big ugly Yankee dyke."

"You read my mind. Mum's the word."

He squared his shoulders, sucked in his cheeks, and marched onto the set. The set consisted of sand, an ocean backdrop, a fake palm tree, and a little thatched hut. Marco leaned against the tree. The tree looked more real. All of a sudden, a props person pulled out a large rubber crocodile and started dragging its mouth over to Marco's ass. Marco looked horrified. The photographer came over sighing with annoyance.

"The idea is we're parodying the famous Coppertone ad. Pull your jeans down."

"But my contract specifically states that there will be no nudity."

"It's not nudity. It's just the top of your ass, just the little part at the top of the crack, which is technically not nudity. It's the cute part. Children love that part. We're not talking about showing your hole here."

"Regardless, I'm not comfortable."

The photographer exhaled deeply. "Wardrobe, could you go in there and see what you can do, please?"

Mary Woodrow from wardrobe entered the ring. She fussed with Marco's waistline as he tried to swat her away. I couldn't understand what was going on. As long as I've known Marco, he was always proud of his body.

Suddenly, the pants were yanked down and Marco screamed. We all saw why—two Carma Norma Bum Pads for Men fell away from his ass and onto the floor. So, that's why he needed privacy. Marco stood there, revealed as a phony. I was shocked. His ass was completely flat. How could I have never noticed before?

This moment was frozen in time until, like a good assistant, I went over and picked up the bum pads and tucked them into the black carryall. As I bent over, the photographer came out of the trance and bellowed at me.

"Who owns that ass?"

"Buddy Cole," I replied sweetly.

"Is it all yours?"

"It was the last time I looked."

"Ever done any modeling?"

"Just at home in front of the mirror."

"So you got lots of experience, then. How would you like to be the new ass of Juicy Mango Jeans?"

"I couldn't. Marco, what do you think?" Marco was in shock and could say nothing. I turned back to the director.

"He wants me to do it."

"Well, let's go, then," the photographer shot back.

Marco was taken to his dressing room by Laughter and Cunt. I slipped into the jeans, and just like Cinderella they fit perfectly. I positioned myself, and the photographer shot miles of film. I was a natural. The entire crew was smitten by my buttocks. First my feet, then my buttocks. My beauty was moving up.

Hours later, I went to get Marco in his dressing room. After all, I was still his assistant. When I found him, he didn't seem upset at all. In fact, he was smiling and laughing. During the time I had been making history, he had been on the phone with his agent and had just been offered a plum modeling assignment in Sweden. He was to leave immediately for an indefinite period of time. All was forgiven. In fact, as far as Marco was concerned, all was forgotten. A psychiatrist would definitely have a field day over my proclivity for choosing a best friend with virtually no short-term memory. Still, Marco seemed unnaturally ebullient. There must have been more to it than that.

"What did you do to him?" I asked the girls.

"We waxed his bikini line," said Cunt.

"Buddy, even the hole," confided Marco. "You never know. The Swedes are very liberal. They might need it in a shot. And after today, I don't want to be caught unawares ever again." I had to agree. So that night, I went home and shaved my own hole. Marco was right. You never knew.

Naturally, the Juicy Mango Jeans campaign was a huge success and soon my likeness adorned flyers from coast to coast. At the height of the hysteria, a huge billboard of me wearing Juicy Mango Jeans went up on the corner of Church and Wellesley, the gay epicenter of Toronto. The reaction was explosive. Soon I was as well-known in the gay community as a bottle of Kwellada.

Downtown luxury living

The day finally came when I moved into my first real apartment, a one-bedroom in a quadraplex above a fish-and-chip store run by a Chinese couple who were also the landlords. I looked around the tiny apartment filled with my possessions—an old tire from an 18-wheeler, a Victrola, a portable bar set, an E-Z Bake oven, the four-hundred-dollar chair—which Marco had given me—a copy of Charles Hix's *Looking Good*, numerous outfits, and of course, Cornygirl. Although at this stage in my relationship with Cornygirl, who really possessed whom?

I was exhausted from moving and collapsed onto the four-hundred-dollar chair. I thought of Marco in Sweden, in the middle of all that blondness, and hoped that it wouldn't numb him to my own blond uniqueness when he returned. Just as I was getting comfortable, I heard a knock at the door. I opened it to reveal a slender, short-haired young woman in jeans and a T-shirt holding a bottle of liquor. She bristled with a boyish energy, and thrust out her hand.

"So, you're the new neighbour, eh?" she said.

"Yes," I replied, shaking her proffered hand.

"I heard noise and I thought it was our landlord, Mr. Kim

Y. Yu, looking for loose change the last tenant might have left behind. She was a meter maid."

"Too bad she wasn't a jeweler," I said.

"I'm Kate Bishop. I'm the lesbian across the way." She held out the bottle. It was a twenty-sixer half-filled with Golden Wedding rye whiskey.

"Welcome Wagon, buddy," she said, and snorted out a laugh. I took the bottle.

"Thanks, that's so nice of you. How did you know my name is Buddy?"

"I didn't. I call everyone buddy."

"Well, then, in order to distinguish me from everybody else, call me Charles." She thought a bit.

"How about Chuck?"

"Chuck it is," I said.

"I'm here to get you drunk, Chuck," she said laughing. Without being invited, she came in and sat on the old tire.

"Where you from?" she asked.

"Quebec."

"Speak some French," she demanded.

"Dépaneur. Entrepreneur. Monsigneur."

"That's pretty good. You speak French like a pro."

We laughed, and sat down with hefty tumblers of the amber elixir. I proposed a toast.

"To my new friend Kate. I'd get into the ring with you, girl."

"To Chuck. Rhymes with fuck." She belted back the rye. There was another knock on the door.

"What is this, Grand Central Station?" I said. We laughed again. There were a lot of good vibrations in the air. I swung open the door to reveal a gay couple, two identical-looking white men in their early thirties, handsome and crisply dressed.

"Hi, we're Tom and Bill, your neighbours. We're teachers

who live next door and we just wanted to bring you a welcome gift," said the slightly taller one.

"I like to play piano. I hope that won't bother you," said the slightly smaller one.

"Here's some potpourri. It's called Summer Sorbet. It'll help take away the fish smell coming from downstairs."

"Now, it's driving me crazy. Which one of you gay blades is Tom and which one is Bill?" I asked.

"I'm Tom. I'm tall."

"And I'm Bill. I'm not so tall."

"I'm Buddy. I'm average height, but that's the only thing average about me." I invited them in. There was another knock. I boldly swept over to the door, which was a foot away, and swung it open. A blinding flash of light hit me. I stumbled back, and when I could see again I noticed a man with a camera stepping toward me. He was a good-looking guy in his early thirties, with dyed black hair curling around his ears. He was wearing a leather jacket, an orange shirt, tight jeans with a classic late seventies basket, Fry boots, a big cowboy belt buckle, and a pierced ear. I was intrigued because I heard that meant you were gay.

"Oh, man, the look on your face." He laughed. "I'm gonna take that picture and put it in a magazine."

"Well, that'll be a first," said Kate sarcastically. "The last time you got a photo in a magazine was a beaver shot in *Oui.*"

"You're just mad that it was yours," he shot back. I was impressed. A real photographer. And a real bastard.

"I'm Peter. My studio's at the end of the hall. I live there. Here, I brought you a gift." He handed me a framed photo of an upside-down pig.

"Thank you. It's beautiful," I said. "I grew up on a pig farm."

"If I was you, I wouldn't be bragging about it. So, where you going to put it?"

"I'll think about it, and put it up later," I said.

"No, put it up now," he snarled. There was steel in his voice.

"Sure," I said. "Where do you suggest?"

"I think it should go right here," he said, pointing to the floor in the dead center of the room.

"On the floor? Won't people step on it?"

"That's the idea," he said. "If people have to avoid stepping on it, it forces them to think about the image." I put the picture on the floor. Kate immediately put her drink on it.

"Kate, are you pregnant?" said Peter. "Last time I had her over for dinner, the turkey baster disappeared." He offhandedly lit a cigarette.

"Tom, Bill. How are you?" he said. "Buddy, can you tell them apart yet? I can't, and I've known them for years. Not only that, but they're both bottoms. Isn't that rich?" he said, blasting through the room.

"And our new tenant, Buddy Cole. I am so pleased to see something fresh behind these cloistered walls. You're certainly an improvement over that meter maid who used to live here. Although she was always good for change. But no mind. And if the dyke is here, the Golden Wedding can't be far behind." He scanned the room and spotted the bottle on the floor.

"Ah, there you are, my golden bride. Cleave to your betrothed." Without asking Kate's permission, he drained the remains of her bottle, then slammed down the empty vessel.

"I've killed her," he said sadly. And then, in high drama mode, he stormed out, slamming the door.

"I hate him," said Tom. Or Bill. The door swung open to reveal Peter once again.

"Oh, by the way, party at my place Friday night. I *will* see you all there. Especially you, Buddy." He left again. We all waited a second in case he was going to burst in again, but he didn't.

"I'm beat. I best be off to bed," said Kate, getting up. "Besides, Peter drank all the booze. Thanks, Chuck." She left, stepping right on the pig's head. Tom and Bill followed her out, muttering, "Good night."

I was finally alone and completely exhausted from the day's events. I liked Kate a lot, and Peter was fascinating. Tom and Bill were a little boring, but they'd be a good audience. I curled up inside the big tire, like water in the rim, and as I dozed off, I remembered that I had never told Peter my name.

*W*anderlust

I was dying in the middle of the desert with nothing but sand for miles of forever. The sun was blinding me. Flies buzzed around the corpse of a camel. My lips were cracked and bleeding from giving head to the bandits who had kidnapped me earlier. And Peter was there, bending over me in a burnoose. His lips were cracked and bleeding, too. I couldn't help but wonder.

"Help me, I need champagne," I croaked.

"I come in, check for cockroach," said Peter, sounding like a gay Chinese man. I opened my eyes. The sun was coming in through the blindless window and someone was banging on the door and screaming in a thick Oriental accent. I sprang out of bed and raced to the door, pulling on my bathrobe. Standing before me was our landlord, Mr. Kim Y. Yu, a slender man wearing gray flannel pants and a white button-down shirt. He appeared agitated.

"Oh it's you, Mr. Yu. How can I help *you*?" I said, laughing. "You must get bored of this."

"Sorry to wake you, Mr. Buddy, but I have to spray room with cock roach powder. Very important must to be do." His voice was charged with almost psychotic repression and I was immediately charmed. His eyes drifted downward and I realized that I was sporting an early morning pee hard-on, which had slipped from the confines of my bathrobe. I casually tucked it back in.

"How's Mrs. Yu?" I inquired good-neighbourly.

"She is very good. She is downstairs. She is waiting for me. It was arranged when we were children. I am very happy husband. Good-bye."

"But Mr. Yu, what about the bug powder?"

"Do yourself. You seem a capable person." He handed me the powder. His eyes darted downward one more time, then he ran off.

I got dressed and decided to go shopping for supplies. I headed off to Kensington Market, a bustling area nearby filled with people from all over the world selling their smelly wares. Bloody foul fowls, great big piles of stinking fish, vaguely obscene roots, and big, crumbly chunks of rank cheese. I loved it. I went right to the butcher and ordered two pounds of pig's feet, a rasher of bacon, and pork liver, which was being given away. Comfort food. Then I thought of Maman, and her pitted, waxy, skin, filled with porky sebaceous pores. Then I thought of Marco, with his matte finish, and his simple diet of basmati rice and greens, and I thought, There's a connection here. Sorry, Maman, I love you, but skin is deeper than blood. I told the butcher to forget the order and moved over to the vegetable stalls.

"Green peppers are marked down six for a dollar," came a voice from behind. It was Kate. She was holding a link of sausages.

"Oh, hi, Kate."

"Hey, look at these sausages I bought." She held them up. They glistened with oily varnish. I began to salivate.

"They look fantastic. Maybe I'll just get a couple. I read somewhere that sausages are supposed to be good for your skin."

"That's my secret, Chuck." We strolled over to the sausage

counter. I ordered a cool dozen, extra fatty. Old habits die hard. Then I asked her about the mysterious Peter, and she told me an interesting story.

"One night, Peter came over and we got to drinkin', and before you know it, he's half in the bag, so I let him sleep on the couch. In the middle of the night I get up to go for a whiz, and I find him shagging some guy in the tub." So he was definitely gay. We parted company, and I continued on my way.

I hopped on the subway and rode north. On my way, I bumped into Tom. Or Bill.

"Oh, hi . . . neighbour. What's up?"

"Nothing," he said. "I've just been shopping for a new globe. The last one we had was destroyed by Peter."

"Really."

"He kicked it off the balcony for a performance-art piece entitled 'Wrecking Your Friends' Apartments.' " This Peter character was becoming more and more fascinating by the minute. I graciously excused myself at the next stop.

I found a mall and went in, ducked through some double doors, and walked down a long hall to a washroom. I went inside. There was a man pretending to dry his hands at the dryer, and another man pretending to wash his hands in the sink. I went to the urinal and began my business. I noticed an old Italian man in a stall, watching me through the crack of the door. I decided to give him a show. I began to stroke myself. His eyes became big as saucers and he did the same. I tried to see what he was sporting and when I did, I was glad. He had a beautiful Italian sausage that put my own purchases to shame. From his waist to his balls, he looked seventeen. I smiled and he turned away. I had forgotten that nothing ruins an anonymous gay encounter more than friendliness.

Then the guy who was washing his hands came over and pretended to take a pee. I noticed his hands were red and chafed from all the washing. He must have been there for hours. I looked down at his penis. It was also red and flaky. That wasn't chafing. It was eczema. Yuck. I returned my eyes frontward. The urinal on my left was now occupied by a slender figure looking the other way. He had jet-black hair and a tight little body. He turned around and looked at me. It was Mr. Kim Y. Yu. He turned beet-red.

"Why me? Why me?" he said.

"No, it's Y. Yu," I corrected.

"I make urine now."

"Me, too. What a coincidence."

"Must go kill cock roach," he sputtered and ran out of the washroom. Damn, I never did get to see his penis.

The man who knew too much

Friday night arrived exactly when I thought it would, at the end of Friday. I had spent the day beautifying myself and by the time I was ready to leave for the party, my face glowed with the power of a thousand roman candles. I took the shine down with a little rice powder and outlined my eyes in kohl. With such a dramatic look, naturally the clothes must follow the face's lead, so I went for an Oriental motif. I chose a quilted satin Mao jacket, the back of which was embroidered with one of those lurid Japanese woodcuts of an overendowed man having sex with two women. Below the waist, I adorned myself with cotton drawstring karate pants, a jade cock ring, and to really make it a show, bound feet. Then, remembering the ultimate rule in fashion, which is to take one thing off before leaving the house, I removed the cock ring.

When Peter swung open the door I was standing with my back to him so he could be greeted by the picture. I heard him laugh. I entered the room backward, turning dramatically to present my striking white face to Peter. He looked impressed. Behind him I could see that the place was filled with a broad range of people.

"I'm surprised there are so many guests here. I saw you more as the solitary type," I said to him.

"I don't know any of these people. I just picked their names out of the phone book."

"Why not just call your friends?"

"I don't have any friends."

"Boo-hoo," I said. "I'm sure your story is sad, Peter, but the real tragedy is that I've been here for almost two minutes and I still don't have a drink in my hand."

"Let's remedy that. What are you drinking?"

"Vodka martini, straight up, olive." He went to get me the drink. I really am intrigued by people's pain, but there's a time and a place. I mean, he's the host of the party, for God's sake. Save the tears till four in the morning.

I saw Kate rolling a joint in the corner, so I skipped over.

"Kate, darling," I said. "Every time I eat sausages and peppers, I am going to think of you."

"You mean, every time you fart, don't you?"

"Oh, Kate, I'm farting now. Give me a hug." She did.

"Let's spark 'er up," she said, lighting the joint. From out of the corner of my eye, I saw Tom and Bill approaching.

"We're so glad to see someone we know," said one of them.

"We don't know anyone here," said the other one.

"I don't either," said Kate.

"Apparently, he just picked names at random out of the phone book," I told them.

"You mean, we're his only friends?" said Kate.

"Apparently."

"Well, I hate him," said Kate.

"We don't like him either," said Tom or Bill.

No one seemed to like Peter, which only piqued my curiosity more. Then I noticed Mr. Kim Y. Yu with an older Chinese woman. I ran up to them.

"Mr. Kim Y. Yu, how are you?" I asked. "How nice of you to bring your mother to the party."

"She is my wife," he shot back.

"We just seem to keep stepping in it when we're around each other, don't we?" I said, laughing coyly.

"My wife can speak no English," he said.

"It's a real shame I didn't get a chance to check you out at the washroom the other day. But I'm sure you'll need to make urine again sometime soon." He smiled, then realizing what I had said, laughed much too loudly. His wife laughed along, too.

"Well, I'm off. Nice meeting you, Mrs. Yu."

I danced away. Now, where was Peter with that drink of mine? I scanned the room and spotted him in the corner kissing a stunning black youth with dreadlocks. That just wouldn't do.

"There you are. I wondered where you'd gone with my drinky-winky." I slipped my arm into Peter's and grabbed the martini and downed it. I was going to need it. Then I turned to the source of my irritation and started to scratch my itch.

"Hello, my name is Buddy Cole."

"The jazz guy?" he asked.

"No, that's Buddy Guy. He plays the guitar. I play the scene."

I turned to Peter. "Come and mingle. Everyone keeps asking who you— I mean, *where* you are."

"I'll be there in a minute," he said.

"But where is 'there'? It could be anywhere. You simply must come now."

"What's going on?" asked the petulant whatever. I moved in for the kill.

"What's going on is that I just saw you kissing my boyfriend." He looked hurt and turned to Peter.

"Jeffrey, you never told me you had a lover."

Jeffrey? I thought. I couldn't resist, so I didn't. "Jeffrey, how could you?" I slapped Peter in the face. He looked pleased. Then, believe it or not, the dreadlocked guy's eyes filled with tears.

"Don't call me," he sobbed, bolting from the room.

"Wow, that was a lot of drama for someone you just met at a party," I said.

"Actually we've been going out for months," Peter replied.

"Oh, well, it looks like I did him a big favour then. As for you, you're obviously doomed. Anyone can see that. But, it's a party, so let's have fun. Oh, and Peter. I really like your friends from the *G* section of the phone book, but the ones from *X* have got to go." And with that, I spun around and ran right into Xingu. He was with my hair and make-up friends, Laughter and Cunt. Their faces seemed younger than before. They had had some work done. I was overjoyed to see him as I really wanted a line of coke.

"Xingu, long time no see. All is forgiven. Let's go to the bathroom. Bring the gals. I don't mind sharing." They followed me. Once inside, Xingu cut four huge rails on the top of the toilet bowl. Cunt pulled a hundred-dollar bill out of her tiny purse and rolled it up. She handed it to me.

"Guests first," she said.

"Thank you, Cunt," I replied. "Coke really does bring out the best in people."

I snorted the blow and passed the bill back to her. She took her allocation, and passed the bill to Laughter. As she leaned over the toilet to do her line, I saw disaster—her long blond mane was about to sweep the cocaine onto the bathroom floor! Without thinking I snatched her hair in my hand and yanked her back roughly. She fell onto the floor.

"What did you do that for?" she cried out.

"Your hair was about to sweep all the goodwill in the room onto the floor."

"You saved the day, man," said Xingu.

"Don't you think I deserve another line?" I asked.

"Yes, I do," I replied, helping myself to my reward. We finished up and rejoined the party. I noticed Mr. Kim Y. Yu standing off in a corner, alone. He looked bombed. I went over and asked him where his wife went. He said she was tired and went home. Then I asked him what had brought him to Canada.

"We come by plane over the water. When I buy the ticket, they ask for credit card, but I only have cash. The woman said that would be okay. So my wife and I go to the passport store and they said they would be ready in one week. So we come back in one week and they are ready. We leave the next day and come here."

"It's true what they say," I said. "Everyone's story is so different. You have a very nice body."

He smiled shyly. "No, no. Is not true."

"I want to see. Let's go into the coatroom and you can take your shirt off and let me be the judge."

"No, no. Am very skinny."

"I don't think so. I think you've got a lot of muscle there," I said, grabbing him playfully.

"Very well," he said, giving in. I followed him into the room where all the coats were piled on a big bed. He moved into the corner and began to awkwardly strip off his shirt. I moved in close and kissed him. He melted in my arms. Literally melted in my arms and slid down onto the floor. He had passed out. I helped him up on the bed, buttoned up his shirt, and with one last kiss, left him to wake up on his own. I snuck back into the party. Let him think it was all a dream.

Smile, you're on *candid camera*

I am in the middle of a virgin Canadian forest. Yves and I are grappling each other bare-chested in front of a group of screaming loggers. I don't know why we are fighting, but with my brothers there never has to be a reason. Yves finally pins me on the ground and then pulls a jackknife out of his breeches, holding the blade to my throat.

"Say uncle," he rasps, his breathing ragged.

"Aunt," I say.

"Don't fucking kid around, Buddy, or I'll kill you."

"*Tante*," I taunt.

"Is everything a joke with you?" he screams, the blade pressing into my windpipe.

"Yes," I reply.

"This is for Papa!" he cries. And then he cuts my throat and I wake up screaming.

I was in my bed. It was the morning after the party. The phone was ringing. It was Peter, telling me to come over right away. I hung up the phone.

When I got to Peter's apartment, Kate, Tom, Bill, and Mr. Kim Y. Yu were there. Peter, however, was nowhere to be seen.

"Where is Peter?" I asked.

"We don't know. The door was unlocked when I arrived first. We haven't seen him yet," said Kate. At that moment, the television came on all by itself. There was a grainy image of a bed with coats piled up on it. I realized with a start that it was the coatroom. Kate appeared on-screen. She came into the room, put her coat on the bed, and started to leave, but then she came back in and began to rifle through someone's coat until she unearthed a wallet. She reached in and pulled out some cash, then put the wallet back. Then she left.

Before any of us had a chance to react, there was an edit, and Tom or Bill came on-screen. Peter's cat was lying on their coats. He tried to get the cat to move, but it refused to budge. Then, out of nowhere, he grabbed the cat by the throat, throttled it, then threw it hard against the wall. The cat ran off, shrieking. He left.

Then, after another edit, Mr. Yu entered the room. I looked over at him as he watched the screen. He looked like he was going to faint again. I looked back and watched myself enter the room. The tawdry little scene played itself out. But how could I feel shame when I looked so amazing on camera?

The next image on-screen was Peter.

"Sorry to get you all up so early on a Sunday morning, but I really feel that the best part of any party is reliving the events of the night before. And why waste time gossiping on the phone all afternoon with lies and exaggerations when you can have it all, *vérité*, right before your very eyes in living colour."

We were all stunned.

"I imagine you're all stunned. I certainly would be. I figured since you all hate me already, why not give you a real reason? So here it is, my gift to you. I'm going away now. I'm tired of these childish games. Buddy, here's how you can tell Tom and Bill apart."

It cut back to the coatroom. Tom and Bill were on the bed with their pants down, necking. The one on the right had a monstrous shlong and the one on the left measured an inch and a half. The scene cut back to Peter.

"Tom is the lucky one, whichever that is. I can't stop having fun. Now, I've got to go. Good-bye." And with that, the tape ended and the television exploded, just like on *Mission: Impossible*.

Everyone skulked back to their apartments. Who was this Peter, and what was this cruel game all about? When I walked inside my place, someone had slipped an envelope under the door. There was a photograph inside.

It was a picture of a boy, about ten years old, standing in front of a barn in the middle of winter, holding a sledge-hammer. The barn was very familiar. I turned the picture over and read what someone had written—PIERRE, 1960. With a shudder I realized that I had found—and lost again—my long-lost brother.

The Art

of

Love

So, let's recap, shall we? I moved to Toronto, became a zombie waiter, starred in a movie, had my own television show, conquered modeling, made two life-long friends, found and lost my brother, and discovered washroom sex. That's not too bad for a piece of Quebec trash, eh?

I had over thirty thousand dollars in the bank, the pick of the boys, and party invitations every night. But life wasn't all mangos, money, and men. What about diamonds? I didn't have one diamond. And what about Peter? Would I ever see him again or would he just remain a ghost in my life? Only time would tell. I also missed Marco tremendously because he was funny, and had great skin. He was an inspiration. Plus, I really needed someone to talk to about gay life's newest wrinkle, AIDS.

Now remember, in the early years of the epidemic, people didn't know anything about AIDS. First they thought it was caused by poppers. So I didn't worry. I didn't do poppers. You see, I'd done a lot of glue growing up on the farm, and trust me, poppers, you aren't glue. Then they said it was from semen. That gave me pause. Then they said it was from being sodomized. That definitely rang a bell.

You see, dear reader, and you are becoming ever dearer to

me, you probably think I'm a classic top—a selfish bully who lives only for his own needs. And it's true, some of those qualities do apply to myself. But I'm actually a pushy bottom and even though I started practicing safe sex early on in the epidemic, let's face it, I'd been getting plowed since I was fifteen. I vowed no more one-night-stands for me. If I was going to continue an active sex life, I had to find one guy to do it with. Yes, my dearest reader, I needed love.

Letter from sweden

After the requisite three-month missing persons' waiting period, Mr. Kim Y. Yu allowed me to move into Pierre's vacant apartment. It was much bigger and was fully furnished. I told only Kate that Peter was my brother. She thought it was best we keep it to ourselves, or as she put it, keep the cops out of it.

What was most odd was that there was nothing in Pierre's apartment to attest to a life lived. It was more an exhibit than an actual apartment. I could find absolutely nothing about our family, or even about Pierre himself. No books, no magazines, not even any food. I didn't even know what my brother's favourite brand of cereal was. The only evidence that my brother had lived there was the telltale Cole male scent on the bedsheets, a heady mixture of cedar, ketchup, freshly cut grass, with a top note of ball sweat. How could my nose have failed me?

One day, a letter arrived from Marco.

Dear Buddy,
I'm prospering here in Sweden. My brunetteness is exotic
and alluring, and I use it to get what I want, which is many
many blond Swedish boys. Kudos all 'round.

Carma Norma came over to visit a couple of weeks ago and we went skiing. I know what you're thinking, Carma Norma on skis? Well, you're right. She never even made it outside. She spent the whole time sitting around the fire with a hot toddy or in her instructor's room, administering to his Swedish needs. He was named, believe it or not, Bjorn, and he was gorgeous, too. Turns out he was a chubby chaser. I was happy for her. However, he gave her chlamydia and it's rendered her sterile. So, some good has come of it. I love Carma dearly but there's no need for progeny.

Tonight I'm going out for dinner with Anika Kjellsen, a makeup girl I met on one of my shoots. She always has coke and isn't too annoying, so that's a blessing.

I've been doing a lot of work, print mostly. One commercial, for a saw called the Thor Saw. Apparently it gives you the strength of a hundred men. I didn't think much of it, but Anika says apparently everyone in Sweden has one, so it's a big deal. Who would have thought it—I'm the Thor Saw guy. Most of the shoots here take place on either a fjord, a sauna, or in an S&M club. That's Sweden for you. The country of extremes. Yet really bland. Sound familiar? The air here is even drier than Canada's, so my pH balance is all over the map. I've been doing a strict combination of Countess Gioella Morning After Restorative Elixir and good old-fashioned donkey milk baths. I have to confess, I no longer use La Ricotta face products even though I am still officially The Face of that infernal mud. The moment I came to Sweden, I broke out. The air here causes a completely different chemical reaction with my skin's mantle. La Ricotta Mud is no good here. I wouldn't use it to clean my boots. I just hope no La Ricotta minions find out about this. Their tentacles don't reach to Sweden yet, but I know it's only a matter of time before I'm exposed. But Buddy, it's worth it for me to have good skin. I can't be a phony.

Well, I've poured my heart out to you. I miss you.

Later, Marco.

I tucked the letter back into my pocket and turned toward Kate, who was busily converting my toilet into a bidet. Kate, who worked as a location scout for movies and TV, was jobless at the time, so I tried to keep her busy. A lesbian without a project is a danger to society.

"Who's the letter from?" she asked.

"My friend Marco, the top model in Sweden I told you about. I can't wait till you meet him."

"Great. Can't wait."

"Kate, what do you do when you're really bored?"

"Chuck, I like to go hunting."

"Hunting? You mean with guns and dead animals and everything?"

"I have this friend, Ralph Schiratti, who I grew up with in Sudbury. We go out hunting together all the time. It just so happens we're going out this weekend."

"Is he cute?"

"I guess so. He's skinny, with a big black beard. He works at Falconbridge Mines." She had my attention, finally.

"You mean he's a miner, with smudges on his face?"

"Well, he washes his face, Chuck."

"But he's not finicky about it."

"Not particularly."

"So what you're saying is, this Ralph friend of yours goes down hundreds of feet under the ground every day with a lamp on his head to toil in the bowels of the earth, and then when he's done, he washes all that grit and grime off in a communal shower with a bunch of other dirty, sweaty miners, many of them uncut? Is that what you're telling me?"

"Yes." Kate was laughing. "And, he's gay." That was the cherry. I couldn't believe how horny the image of Ralph in a mine made me.

"Kate, would you like some company this weekend?"

"Oh, I see. Okay. This could be fun."

"Great. Watch out, Bambi," I said. "Kate, can you hurry up fixing that thing? I need to go for a crap."

"I'm done. But now that I've turned your toilet into a bidet, where will you go?"

"Just mind your own business." She stepped out as I pushed my way inside and closed the door. Two minutes later, I reappeared, fresh as a daisy.

"Could you fix the sink?" I asked. "There seems to be a clog."

Northward bound

On Saturday morning, we loaded up Kate's pickup truck and drove north. I was really looking forward to getting out of the city again. About an hour after we left Toronto, the highway became dense with evergreens. The landscape began to roll with hills, and lakes began to appear. Soon, outcroppings of rock could be glimpsed here and there, and eventually the rock surface crowded right to the side of the road, like big curtains slowly closing in at the end of a show. We were entering the Canadian Shield.

About four hours later, the trees suddenly began to thin until there was almost no vegetation but lichen, clinging to the black rocks that were everywhere.

"What happened to all the trees?" I asked, mystified.

"It's the pollution from all the mines. Welcome to Sudbury. That's why they built that," she said, pointing to a towering chimney looming on the horizon. "Their solution for the pollution was to build a giant smokestack, the biggest in the world, that would send all the smoke so high into the stratosphere that it wouldn't come down again until Cincinnati." She laughed.

"It looks like the surface of the moon. Not that I've been there yet."

"In the seventies, NASA used to train their astronauts here because it was the one place on Earth that most resembled the moon."

"The moon's less forbidding," I said, looking around.

Ralph lived at the base of Big Nickel Hill, which was a hill with a statue of a big nickel on top of it. There was also a big dime and a big penny. Sixteen big cents. I hoped some giant didn't come along and scoop it up.

We drove up the driveway to his house, a little bungalow with aluminum siding, a porch, the standard ivy and rose-bushes, a carport, and for some reason, a half-shingled roof. Sure enough, behind the house loomed a giant nickel on top of a hill, if a nickel could be said to "loom." The door opened and Ralph came out. I felt like I was finally looking at the future Mr. Cole.

He was small and wiry, in a white T-shirt with the sleeves cut off, big green army pants with giant pockets, and black Canadian army boots. He had black hair to his shoulders, cut like a lesbian pageboy but sexy on him. His full black beard and dark haunted eyes made him look like Rasputin in a porno movie.

"Hey, Kate," he said, leaning into the car. I caught a whiff of his b.o. It was the smell of a man who'd been reading *HAWG* magazine all day in his basement under a black light poster of KISS. I found it intoxicating. "So, you're Buddy, eh? I'm Ralph. Come on in. You hungry?"

"I'm famished," I said, getting out of the car. "Kate was a slave driver. Never let us stop once. Made me wear a catheter. Where can I empty this?" I said, holding up a bag. Poor Ralph couldn't tell if I was joking or not. I knew he'd be a lot of fun to tease.

"We can go out hunting, as soon as we try my grandma's strudel. She would be very hurt if we didn't." Ah, a boy who loves his grandma. I never thought of that as being sexy before. This boy was rewriting all the rules.

"Well, I've never hurt a grandmother yet and I certainly don't intend to start now," I said, and grabbed Ralph's arm in a flirty Auntie Mame manner. He flinched and pulled away.

"It's just my grandma's from the old country and everything so, you know."

"I understand. I'm from Quebec. She doesn't know you're gay?" I said.

"Oh, she knows." He smiled and looked at Kate. She snickered.

"What was that all about?" I asked.

"Nothing. Let's go in," said Ralph. We walked inside. The house was filled with little trinkets from Italy and Blue Mountain Pottery. At the end of the hall, an older, stout woman in a flowered dress and clean apron was toiling over an enameled stove, pulling a large strudel out of the oven. I had a vision of Maman turning from the stove with a hot *tortière* and I felt a rush of emotion. She faced us, holding the pan in front of her. Her huge arms wobbled with the effort.

"Come in, bring your friend, Ralphie. Introduce." She had a sad Italian accent.

"It's me, Mrs. Schiratti. Kate."

"Ah, *sì*, Kate. You still a girl-girl?"

"Yeah," Kate replied gay-pridely. Grandma Schiratti sighed deeply and then turned her baleful gaze on me.

"Who you?"

"Buddy Cole, ma'am."

"What you do?"

"I'm a model." Well, I was. Sure, I'd only had one job, but it was prestigious.

"So you are gay, too."

"Definitely not," I replied brightly. Kate did a double take. I could feel the devil rising in me. This was going to be delicious.

"That's good. Ever since my Ralphie told me he like boys, I

have been dead inside. Better to shoot me with a gun than tell me that."

"Nonna, don't start," said Ralph, with impossibly cute embarrassment that turned me on to no end. I love when people are ashamed of their loved ones. There are so many buttons to push.

"Buddy, why is such a good-looking young man like you still single?"

"Me? What about you?" I told her.

"Long time for me," she said, flirtatiously.

"Use it or lose it," I told her.

"*Che banite*," she said, which is Italian for *adorable scamp*, or something.

"Ahhhhh, is so hot, Buddy, and the summer she just begin. And there are no trees, so there is no shade. Lotsa gays. But no trees. That's why I cannot sleep all night," she said, plopping herself into a kitchen chair.

"Do you have insomnia, dear?" I asked in the manner of a caring nursing-home assistant.

"I can no sleep, Buddy. Every night I dream the Big Nickel roll off the hill, and I must push back up to the top. So I push, but is heavy, and I struggle, but I do. Then the Big Nickel roll down the hill again, and I must do all again. Have some strudel." I dug in. It tasted just like Maman's.

"Buddy, you are good boy," Grandma Schiratti said to me. "Talk to Ralph. Make him change. In your business, you must know many beautiful girls."

"I will do everything in my power to make sure that a beautiful model ends up in your grandson's arms," I said. No one said it had to be a girl. I looked over at Ralph, who was suppressing a laugh. It made his neck veins stand out in stark relief, making me wish I was a real vampire, not just as glamorous as one.

"Thank you, Buddy," she said, her hand to her breast and her eyes filled with Old World tears. "You so kind. Good night, everyone. I try to sleep now. Kate, I hope you baptize before you do anything." She tottered off to her room. The moment she left, we all burst out laughing.

"I couldn't believe it when you said you weren't gay," stammered out Kate over her laughter.

"It's possible." I felt the need to defend the indefensible. Like my support for O. J.

"I could see you as straight, Buddy," said Ralph quietly. I immediately became aroused. Why did it turn me on for him to see me as straight? Who cares, it worked. It unnerved me so much I actually blushed and had to look away, and when I looked back at Ralph, he was blushing, too, above the beard line. My, oh, my. There was more blushing going on than a bride on poppers. Sensing the romantic tension in the air, Kate suggested we get a move on, and we got ready for the hunt.

We squeezed into Ralph's battered pickup truck. I sat beside him and he let me work the gears while he drove. We went about twenty miles out of town and turned down a dirt road, where we parked and got out in the middle of nowhere. Ralph took out a can of Off insect repellent and covered his arms and legs. Then he covered his face as Kate sprayed his head. Then he sprayed her. After which Ralph offered me the Off, but I declined. I was saturated in Avon's Skin So Soft, and I don't know what it is, but whenever I put it on, insects stay away. Now everyone uses it as insect repellent and I don't see a dime. Ralph stuck his finger in his mouth and held it up to the wind. I thought of those falling asses again.

"What are we going to kill, anyway?" I asked.

"Rabbit," said Kate, running off ahead.

"Not Bugs Bunny!" I cried in mock horror. "Ralph, you wouldn't kill Bugs Bunny, would you?"

"No. Just his relatives," he joked back.

"Oh, Ralph," I said, and tripped on a leaf, so as to fall against him. I took his arm as before and this time he didn't shake me off. It felt like iron through his shirt. I looked around.

"We seem to have lost Kate."

"We'd better find her. It's dangerous to lose sight of one another," he said.

"Just relax. Let me comb your beard."

"I don't know," he said hesitantly.

"Come on, it'll be fun."

"Okay," he said. I took out a comb and started grooming his facial hair.

"That feels terrific," he said. I went and sat down next to a tree.

"Come here, put your head in my lap." He did so. His head balanced perfectly atop my erection, like identical twins on a teeter-totter.

"Relax your neck muscles."

"If I do, I'll fall off your penis."

"That's okay, I'll catch you." He let his head fall and lay his cheek against my teeter-totter as I continued combing.

"Has anyone ever combed your beard before?" I cooed.

"You mean besides my grandmother?" The blood rushed from my penis.

"Do you use conditioner?" I asked him, changing the subject.

"No, just soap and water."

"Well, your beard is in very good shape," I said. "Virtually no split ends."

"I guess it hasn't been roughed up in a while," he said looking up at me with a sexy, sly look. I had to look away. The next time, I would hold his gaze.

"My father used to hunt," I told him.

"Did you ever go with him?"

"Sure, all the time. Someone had to prepare lunch."

"Did you ever shoot anything?"

"Sure."

"A rabbit?" he asked.

"No. My brother Davide. I only wounded him, though. He claimed it was deliberate, but why would I want to kill my much-hated gay brother?"

"I can't see you doing anything like that. You're a good person, Buddy Cole."

"Well, I'm fabulous, but I'm not good."

"I think you're good." And that did it. No one had ever called me "good" before. I looked down at his ruby red lips, which were peeking out through his black beard. Then I leaned down and kissed him. It was the greatest kiss of my life, because for the first time it was more than just lust. It was lust with a beard. Who knew that could add up to love?

"Can I comb out your pubic hair?" I asked, unbuttoning his pants. Without waiting for an answer, I reached inside. I'd never felt such urgency before. His four-inch erection exploded in my palm. Not exactly a Falcon video. Somehow, it didn't matter.

"I'm sorry," he said.

"That's okay. There's more to love than a big dick and someone who can go all night. That's where I come in. See how we fit together?" Wedding bells began to clang in my head. They say you can't move too quickly when it's the right time. Before we could discuss the wedding plans Kate broke the spell, reappearing out of nowhere.

"Hey, somebody's getting busy," said Kate, coming toward us. "Better be careful. Some hunter might mistake you two guys for fags and shoot you." We buttoned up. She was carrying a large rabbit by his ears in one hand, and a dead duck in the other. "Look what I got. Bugs and Daffy."

"We don't have a license for duck hunting," said Ralph, standing up.

"Who are you? Department of Natural Resources? Let's go home and cook some Looney Tunes."

When we arrived back at the house, Grandma Schiratti's

eyes popped when she saw the spoils of the hunt. She grabbed the game from Kate's hand and slapped the beasts down on the counter.

"Nice duck and rabbit. Who shoot?"

"I did," replied Kate, huntress-pridely.

"I'm no surprise." She turned to me. "Now, I work. Buddy, you want to watch?"

"I'd love to." Kate and Ralph went down to his basement bedroom to listen to music and I stayed behind. I felt it was important to get on her good side. I knew that the best way to an Italian boy's heart was through his grandmother.

She took a pair of blunt scissors, cut the duck's neck, and bled it into the sink. Then she put a large pot of water on the stove to boil. While we waited she went after the rabbit. She did the same to it and by the time it was all bled the water was boiling. She dropped the duck carcass into the boiling water for a minute, and then fished it out.

"Now the feathers will come off so easy." She pulled a few out. "See."

"I do. You're very good." She smiled as she ripped out the bird's plumage. Then she grabbed a large knife and cut the breastplate open. She reached inside the duck's body and began pulling out the entrails. Its intestines seemed to go on forever.

"Look, Buddy," she said. She was holding up a severed duck foot. She pulled on a small nerve ending, which made it clench and unclench. I jumped back and she roared with laughter. She held it in my face and laughed even louder. Soon she was chasing me around the kitchen with it, shrieking with joy like a little boy dangling a frog in his sister's face. I screamed with mock fear. Eventually, I became winded, but Grandma still looked good for another lap. God bless pasta.

"Maybe we should get back to work," I suggested. The sexual tension was so thick you could cut it with bloody, blunt scissors. Everyone in this family wanted me.

We returned to dead Daffy. She dug back in and pulled something out. "These are for you," she said, holding out several small yellow duck yolks in the palm of her hand.

"What do I do with them?"

She got out two glasses and set them down. "One for me," she said, sliding one yolk into a glass, "and one for you," she continued, putting the other yolk into the other glass. Then she grabbed a bottle of Marsala from the cupboard and poured a jigger in each glass.

"Don't tell Ralphie." She winked, holding up the bottle. "Maybe it chase away bad dream and I can sleep." She held her glass up for a toast.

"To Ralph and the beautiful model," I proposed.

"I drink to that." And we downed it. I felt like Sylvester Stallone in *Rocky*, except I don't think he slipped off to the washroom afterward to puke. "Where's Ralph's parents, Nonna?"

"Oh, Buddy, sad story. My son Romaldo he was good man. Always fix thing. Good to his mamma. He fall off the roof and die." That accounted for the half-shingled roof.

"What about the mother?"

"Oh, her. She is in Rouyn. French slut! She has been re-marry five, six time. Every man have her. Even the Indian." I hoped Ralph took after his mum.

Hours later we were sitting around the dining room table, finishing a sumptuous feast of rabbit, duck, roast potatoes, iceberg lettuce drenched in oil and vinegar, and Pepsi to wash it all down.

"That was the best rabbit stew I've ever tasted," Kate said.

"Hmmm," responded Grandma with a chill. "What about you, Buddy? You like?"

"Quackingly good." She beamed at me.

"Let me help you clean up, Grandmother Schiratti," offered Kate.

"Sit down," she said. "I can do myself. Buddy, you give me hands?"

The two of us cleared the table and did the dishes, chatting the whole time. Kate and Ralph went to the rec room to watch the hockey game. The Toronto Maple Leafs had declared war on the Montreal Canadiens or something. I would rather do dishes with an old woman than sit through that. After the dishes were done, we sat around the kitchen table drinking perked coffee and chatting. Soon, we heard the TV go off and Kate and Ralph reappeared in the kitchen door. They seemed sad. I guess Montreal had won.

"Fucking Leafs," muttered Kate.

"Kate, no swear. This is no some lezzie pool hall," warned Grandma Schiratti.

"I'm sorry," she said.

"Me, I'm tired," said Grandma. "I go lie down, maybe sleep one two minute before the dream start. Buddy, where you sleep?"

"I can crash on the couch, here."

"No, no. You are guest. Ralph, be nice. Offer Buddy your bed."

"Buddy, would you like to sleep in my bed?" asked Ralph impishly.

"I'd love to," I said, completely giving it away. Although by this time Grandma Schiratti was so besotted with love for me that I could have pulled out a gun and wiped everybody out, and she would say they had driven me to it.

"*Buono serra*. Tomorrow, I make nice breakfast." She left the room.

"How the hell does she know lesbians play pool?" asked Kate.

"I watch *60 Minutes*," came her voice from down the hall. We waited until we were sure she was out of earshot.

"Sorry she's so mean to you, Kate," said Ralph.

"It's all right. She just doesn't know she's a dyke yet."

"Oh, you think everybody's gay," said Ralph, defending his grandmother like a good Italian boy. Go, *paisan*!

"Well, everybody in this room is," I said. "That's one hundred percent. Case closed. Anyway, I'm exhausted," I said, rubbing my belly.

"Why are you rubbing your belly?" asked Kate.

"Oh, right. Wrong gesture," I said, stretching and yawning. She took the hint.

"Well, I've had enough excitement for one day. I'm going to sleep," she said, getting up and going outside.

"Where are you going, Kate?" asked Ralph.

"Gonna sleep in the back of the truck," she said. "Don't mind."

"Sleep topless and pretend you're at the Michigan Womyn's Festival," I suggested.

"Have fun, boys," she laughed, and went outside. I followed Ralph downstairs into his room. It was covered with brown paneling and rock posters. There was a milk crate bookshelf, a workout area with an incline bench and free weights, a Ping-Pong table, a beanbag chair in front of a small TV, and above a huge water bed, an elaborate stereo system. When I got closer, I noticed two large starfish and a Styrofoam wig head with speakers built into them.

"This is cool," I said, taking it all in.

"The starfish are the tweeters, and the wig head is the woofer."

"I'm not much of an audiophile myself. My requirement for a stereo is an off-and-on switch."

"So you're not very mechanical?" he asked.

"Are you kidding? I can barely operate a hammer. On the other hand, I could make a martini in a twister."

"We had a twister here once."

"That must have been exciting. Did anyone die?"

"Nope."

I immediately lost interest. "Ralph, put something romantic on this futuristic supersonic sexaphonic stereo system of yours." He brightened and ran over to a milk crate of LP's and put a record on. "Broken Wings" by Mister Mister came blaring out. Ralph commanded me to lie down on the water bed and put my head between the two starfish for maximum effect. I did so and was engulfed in a wall of sound. I totally overplayed it for Ralph, writhing about in the throes of aural ecstasy, causing waves in the waterbed.

My Anita-Eckberg-lost-at-sea routine seemed to turn him on immensely. He took off his shirt and lay down on the water bed beside me. We stared at each other through the waves. Sometimes, it got so rough I'd lose him at the bottom of a trough and then spy him again at the crest. Eventually the sea settled and we managed to exchange a kiss, but this set the ocean off again. It went on like this almost all night until we realized that it wasn't going to work and ended up blowing each other in the bathroom.

At long last, love

The next morning I awoke with a song in my heart, but nausea in my stomach from spending the night at sea. I looked over at Ralph, who was slowly waking up. His hair was an unruly broom, his eyes were swollen and bloodshot, his beard was completely flattened on one side, and the pattern of the bedspread was pressed into his face. He looked adorable.

"Breakfast ready!" bellowed Grandma's voice from upstairs. We dressed each other and went up. She had prepared a huge spread—bacon, eggs, toast, coffee, tea, pancakes, ham, leftover duck, dried prunes, chocolate cake, and again, lots of Pepsi.

"You got enough food?" she asked me. "I can make you nice grill cheese."

"No, this is plenty. I don't intend to eat all of it. I'll give Kate a prune." She squeezed my cheek.

"Did you sleep last night?" I asked her.

"For one minute, maybe."

"Did you have the dream during that minute?"

"Yes. Only take forty second."

"You must be moving up that hill. Anyway, I'm full," I said, stretching and yawning. Kate looked at me like I was losing my mind. And I was. I looked over at Ralph. He was eating like a pig, and his underarm hairs were soaked. The smells of meat and sweat invaded my nostrils. I lost a thousand more brain cells.

"What are you doing today?" asked Grandma.

"I'm taking Kate and Buddy for a tour of the mine," said Ralph through a mouthful of chocolate cake.

"No fall down hole," chortled Grandma. "I try go sleep again."

We jumped into Kate's truck and drove to the mine. We went through the security gate and parked, then walked a long way to a tiny guardhouse. A big man greeted us.

"Hey, Ralph. These your friends?"

"Yeah, Gerry. This is my friend Buddy and his wife, Kate," said Ralph, giving me a wink. Kate blanched, but held back. "They want a tour of underground."

"Sure, okay. Why don't you folks put on these things," he said, handing us hardhats and safety glasses.

"What size shoe do you take?" he asked me, pulling down some safety boots.

"Ten," I said. "And the little lady here takes a perfectly darling five. Half my size. Perfect husband-wife ratio." Kate gave me her "you're pushing it" look. Then the guy handed Ralph and me white coveralls, and Kate was handed pink ones. That sent her over the edge.

"So the idea is, hubby, white is the most visible in the dark, but because of some archaic patriarchal bullshit, I have to wear pink, because I'm a woman which makes me less visible," she barked. I glanced over at Ralph, who looked extremely uncomfortable in front of his straight coworkers. I went into spin control.

"Okay, here's the scenario, darling. There's a mining disaster. Hundreds are buried in the rubble. A rescuer comes across two people trapped under a beam. One of them is in a pair of white coveralls, the other is in pink. He has only seconds to save one of them before the roof gives way. It's *Sophie's Choice* time. Nine times out of ten, that man will go for the pink. Right, boys?" The miners burst into applause.

"I know I do." I looked at Kate.

"Now do you feel safe?" She said nothing. I looked over at Ralph. He looked like he was going to die of embarrassment. I wished Kate would stop acting so dykey. We put on our outfits and waited with the rest of the men.

The elevator arrived, and all thirty of us filed in. It dropped suddenly and began to hurtle downward. My ears popped, and I felt a sudden stab of claustrophobic terror. For a moment, I forgot where I was and clung on to Ralph for dear life.

"Honey, why are you clutching that man's arm when I'm your wife?" asked Kate wickedly. I brought my arms to my side with great dignity as every back in the elevator stiffened. The goodwill from my pink speech had dried up. We rode to the bottom silently.

We finally reached our destination, ten thousand feet below the surface—a long dark corridor of rock. The only illumination came from the lamps on our hats. Ralph led us in a direction away from the other men.

"Come on, I'll show you where I work," he said, taking us to a pile of rocks. "I take the raw iron ore from over here and shovel it onto this conveyor belt and it goes out to the other side of the mine. Eleven dollars and forty cents an hour. Unless I get overtime, but that doesn't happen unless the belt goes down, then you have to move it with a wheelbarrow. It's a good job."

Kate held her tummy and grabbed my arm. "Honey, I think I'm having my period," she said. "I know how much that grosses you boys out, so I won't go into details. Is there a bathroom?"

"Yeah, we got a Johnny-on-the-spot over there," indicated Ralph.

"Don't fuck my husband while I'm gone," she said to Ralph as she jogged away.

"Women!" I said. "Ralph, that rock over there looks comfortable. Let's go sit down."

We went behind a big rock and made out while Kate did whatever she did. After about fifteen minutes, I realized that she wasn't coming back.

"Do you think we should go looking for her?" I asked.

"I haven't come yet."

"Oh, you're adorable," I said, and continued to deep-throat him, which wasn't difficult. An hour later, he still hadn't come. The first time, he came instantly. Now he couldn't come at all. That's what I think I loved about Ralph—variety.

"Shouldn't we be getting back?" I asked, finally giving up. "It's getting dark." Ralph laughed. I laughed. We became hysterical, the joyous sound echoing throughout the mine. I imagined our love laughter moving through layers of igneous and sedimentary rock, down into the primordial layer where the fossils lie, deeper and deeper, finally bursting through into the molten core at the center of our beautiful planet, making the magma bubble with glee.

"God, you can hear you guys from the center of the earth." Kate had returned. "Let's go. I've got cramps," she said, stomping off.

"I thought they turned nice once their little friend arrives," I said to Ralph.

When we returned home, the table was set and something was cooking in the oven. The place smelled like an enchanted cottage. But there was something else amidst the savoury smells. Something sickly sweet. Cloying and vaguely funereal. The old dame was wearing perfume. Suddenly, she swept into the kitchen wearing a brightly coloured dress.

"Nonna, why are you all dressed up? Did somebody die?" asked Ralph.

"I just fix my hair," she said.

"Nonna, you're wearing a Wonderbra." It was true. Her breasts looked like torpedoes.

"Buddy, you have good day today?" she said, bustling about the stove. "You go under the ground?"

"Yes, it was very exciting. Did you get any sleep?"

"No, no sleep, but I do pretty good for no sleep, no?" she said, leaning forward on the table flirtatiously and squeezing her bosom together with her big baker's arms.

"I love your cameo," I said, her breasts in my face. "I can see every detail."

"My husband give to me, long long long time ago, when I was girl."

"You're still a girl. Or at least you look like one tonight."

"You think?" She blushed. She poured us each a glass of wine.

"My husband make the wine, Ralphie's nonno. Him be so shame if he see what Ralphie become." She suppressed a sob. "But we can drink."

The wine was pure vinegar, but we all pretended it was delicious. The meal was inedible, but we ate it anyway. She had obviously spent so much time on her hair and makeup that she had neglected what was really important—our stomachs. Grandma Schiratti didn't notice. She was too busy drinking Nonno's wine. By the end of the meal she had emptied the bottle and was falling out of her dress. Finally she collapsed on the table, asleep. Everyone held their breath. Kate poked her arm. She didn't move. Ralph looked stunned.

"Well, she's been asleep for more than a minute. That's her personal best," I said. Ralph and I picked her up and brought her to her room. When we placed her in the middle of the bed, the mattress was so soft that she sunk to the bottom and disappeared into the folds of old-lady bedding.

"Well, there's her problem right there," I said to Ralph. "She needs a firmer mattress. What is it with your family and bad mattresses? You guys are a chiropractor's dream." We decided to end the day by hiking up Big Nickel Hill. It was very steep and when we finally got to the top, we were winded. We held each other up as we regained our breath. The five-cent leviathan loomed before us, glittering in the light of a full moon.

"Imagine the size of the gum ball," I wondered aloud. Ralph said nothing, just took my hand and led me over to the base of the monument. We looked up. It was a beautiful night—millions of stars dotted the inky blackness.

"It's so romantic," I said. "Me, you, the moon, a giant nickel."

"This is where I come when I want to be alone."

"Do you want me to leave?" I asked teasingly.

"No, no," said Ralph. "Stay."

"I'm kidding. You take everything so seriously."

"I'm sorry. I'm boring, eh?"

"No, you're not boring. I think you're wonderful. I don't go for boring people." I leaned in and kissed him. We began to make love. Overcome by the beauty of the surroundings and love for this taciturn miner, I asked Ralph to take me in the way the poets wrote about. He agreed. There was only one snag.

"Do you have a condom?" I asked.

"What? I'm not going to make you pregnant."

"Haven't you ever heard of safe sex?"

"Oh, you mean AIDS. Only old guys get that. You're not that old."

"You're right. Just pull out before you come."

I figured he was from Sudbury so I was probably safe. Nothing ever happened there. Just as the plane was at the hangar door, something big and soft fell over us. It was Grandma Schiratti. She must have been sleepwalking up the hill. But she wasn't sleepwalking anymore. She stared with horror at the scene, as we frantically tried to make ourselves decent.

"Ralph, how could you? You turned Buddy into a gay. Why? Why?" she wailed.

"Let me handle this," I said to Ralph. "Grandma Schiratti, this isn't real. This is a dream."

"A dream?"

"Yes. You're asleep right now. And here's what happens in the rest of the dream. Ralph and I walk you down the hill. Then we tuck you into your cozy little bed, and you fall into the most restful sleep of your life. And when you wake up in the morning, you will completely accept your grandson's homosexuality. And, you're going to buy yourself a new mattress." Then we walked her down the hill toward the house. Finally, we were back in her room.

"Hop in," I said, "and this time, stay put." She sat on the edge of the bed with a demented smile.

"If this is dream, I can have what I want, no?"

"Sure."

"I want you to kiss me good night," she said. Ralph looked away uncomfortably as I leaned in and placed a gentle kiss on her papery lips. Then she pulled me toward her and slipped me the tongue. What the hell, it's her dream. I'd have done a lot more.

"I can sleep now," she said. With that, she fell into a deep slumber and began to snore. Later that night, Ralph and I watched *Saturday Night Live* in bed and shaved each other's balls. We had become an old gay married couple in the course of one weekend. I had never been happier.

The next morning when we got up, Grandma was still asleep. We had coffee and toast in the kitchen. We lingered at the table holding hands. Neither of us knew what to say. Kate was outside packing the truck. I had to make my move.

"Ralph, why don't you come with us?" I said with an unfamiliar note of desperation creeping into my voice. I didn't like it one bit, but I couldn't help myself.

"To Toronto? Why? I'd have nothing to do there."

"There's lots to hunt. Squirrels, raccoons, skunks. There's a new bathhouse in town called The Cellar. It's just like being underground. There's nothing here for you."

"What are you talking about? I got the whole rec room to myself. I got my stereo. Cable TV. Nonna cooks for me. I got the woods right outside my door. What more do I need?" This was it. I was finally ready to say the word.

"Love," I ventured. He looked away, embarrassed.

"You don't love me, do you?" I asked. He was quiet. I exploded.

"After all I've done for you. After all the doors I've opened!"

"Buddy, we met two days ago."

"You obviously haven't read my book!" I snapped. "Things happen very quickly in *Buddy Babylon*. Fine! I'll write you out of this chapter. There will be no reincorporation for you." I tilted my chin up, scrambling to regain my dignity.

"Well, I'm off. I'm sure Kate will want to beat the traffic." I walked outside, not looking back, and got into the passenger seat of the truck. Kate was behind the wheel.

"What did you do? Tell him you're in love with him?"

"Just drive!" I commanded. Ralph leaned into the driver's-side window.

"See you next year, Kate," he said. "That was fun." I stared off in pain.

"I really liked meeting you, Buddy."

"You're a heartbreaker, Ralph! You've ruined me for other people. I just want you to know that. And, I had a really good time." We hit the road. The drive home was quiet, except for one outburst—

"Would you turn off those goddamn Indigo Girls? If I have to listen to one more lesbian lament about lost love, I'm getting out of this car and walking to the nearest gay bar to suck everyone off!" After that, there was complete silence till we got back to Toronto. Kate let me off wordlessly.

In the weeks following, I just drifted about my apartment wearing nothing but a pair of tights and a cape. Sleep came rarely, and when it did I was tormented with dreams of a giant nickel and singing starfish. I felt the pain that only Shakespearean characters must feel and for the first time ever, I thought about killing myself, but couldn't find an asp. After years of escaping virtually unscathed from one affair after another, my heart had finally been broken. By a nerdy miner with b.o. Not exactly a Danielle Steel novel.

Rhapsody in fur

Another letter arrived from Marco.

Dear Buddy,

So much has happened since I last wrote. Where do I start? One night, Anika and I did three grams of blow and I really opened up to her. I told her all about my disillusionment with La Ricotta, and she really seemed to understand. The next day, while cutting the hair of the wife of the president of La Ricotta who was visiting from Milan, Anika let it slip that I didn't use the products in my own personal life. The bitch told her husband, and the dominoes began to fall. Needless to say, I've lost my contract, and I'm freelancing once again. But all is not lost. Yesterday some bigwig from Ikea was here and spoke to me about a potentially lucrative offer modeling bookshelves.

I've been seeing someone. He's Swedish, with long blond hair. His name is Bikvi Op. I know, what kind of a name is that? It doesn't matter, though, because he has huge goddamn balls. And that's what really counts. It's true what they say— Swedes are all balls. And you know how I feel about balls. They're roundness's greatest moment.

Anyway, I'm having a good time. And that's all that matters. I hope you're having a good time, too. I hope you've gotten some work. You're a beautiful human being in more ways than one. And not just physically, but facially, too. And remember, you're a natural blond. How many people can say that? Well, everyone in this country. People tell me you're brilliant, and I believe it, because I'm a good judge of other people's judgments.

Well, that's about it for now. I hope life is treating you well. Please write me, Buddy. I know you have a hard time putting pen to paper, but this is Marco!

See you soon. I miss you and Canada.

Love and kisses, Marco.

Marco's letter cheered me up tremendously. At least he was there for me. Gay love was obviously a no-win situation, but gay friendship was at least a possibility. I couldn't stop thinking about Ralph. Maybe that's because I had grown a beard since we broke up. Everyone hated it, but I couldn't have cared less what they thought. Sometimes, late at night, lying in the darkness, I'd numb my face with novocaine and stroke my beard, pretending all the while that I was touching Ralph's face. I masturbated like this for months. If I couldn't have the man I wanted, I'd become the man I couldn't have.

Why did I love Ralph? Oh, sure, I found him terribly attractive, but it's not like the sex was unbelievable. I had had better sex with people I hated. But still, Ralph Schiratti could not be shaken loose from my brain. From my soul. From my beard.

One day, Kate came over. She had spoken to Ralph about some sort of darts competition they were planning to attend, and according to Kate he only mentioned me once, in passing. I was incensed. Why didn't he at least call me? Kate reminded me that I had a dialing finger, too. So one night, after two too many martoonis, and after watching an episode of *The Red Fisher Show*, I phoned him. Grandma Schiratti answered. She told me about her new mattress, and then talked in glowing terms about Ralph's new boyfriend. My post-hypnotic suggestion had worked. Damn! I told her I was dating an actress and hung up. I fell to the floor in a swoon and lay there for four days, only getting up to wash, dress, eat, use the bathroom, and make phone calls. On the fourth day, Kate came over to shake me out of my stupor of sorrow.

"It's your fault! He was your friend!" I shrieked.

"Look, I just introduced you. I didn't tell you to fall in love with him. Besides, you just got caught up in the romance of Sudbury. Happens to people all the time. If you had met him in the back room of The Barn at a Sunday tea dance, you'd have forgotten him by Monday."

"That's not true. I love him."

"Ah, Chuck. Ralph's into his own thing. It ain't gonna happen. Find someone else."

"I don't work like that. I am pure emotion. I could fall in love with Hitler. That's just who I am."

"Look, Chuck, you've been cooped up here for two weeks. Let's go for a walk." We left the apartment and walked down the street. It was the first time since my exile that I had been outside. People didn't seem to care about my problems. Many of them were smiling. Some of them even had kites.

We passed the Royal Ontario Museum, where I had spent many an hour looking at dinosaur exhibits and Egyptian bric-a-brac. What else is there in a museum? We decided to go around the back and smoke a joint. I hadn't been high in ages. We hid behind a Dumpster, and Kate lit up a huge doobie. Before I knew it, I felt great. Kate decided to look in the Dumpster and discovered a huge, stuffed grizzly bear that had seen better days. Even after death.

We jumped into the Dumpster and wrestled the bear out. It weighed a ton, but Kate was a lesbian and I had a mission, so we were strong enough. We carried it on our shoulders all the way back to the apartment. Oddly enough, no one on the street said a word. Toronto is so pathetic. We could have led a nude Cher down the street on a leash and no one would have said anything.

We placed the bear in my front room. I called him Borgnine, after Tova. He helped with my loneliness, and time crawled on. Soon, the snow began to fly, and I huddled indoors with my ursine lover. The only drama was the constant bickering between Cornygirl and Borgnine.

One bitter winter's day, Carma Norma came by to visit. In the absence of Marco, we clung to each other. I don't think we really liked each other very much, but she always brought gifts and never overstayed her welcome. When she walked in, I gasped. She was wearing a massive, full-length white fur coat. It was the first thing she had ever worn that looked any good on her.

"I love your new coat! What is it?"

"It's polar bear, Marco's friend."

"Carma, I insist you call me Buddy. Even strangers do."

"Slow down. I can't handle intimacy," she said. She braced herself. "Okay. It's polar bear . . . Buddy."

"That wasn't so hard. Now, Carma, show my new friend Borgnine how gorgeous his cousin's pelt looks on you."

"What new friend?" she asked.

"There," I said, motioning to the corner. Carma noticed the bear and let out a panicky yelp.

"Whatthefuckisthat?" she screeched.

"That's Borgnine. I think he's offended by your coat."

"Well, mine's a polar bear," she said defensively.

"Are you saying grizzly bears are inferior to polar bears? Carma, what a racist," I said accusingly. "Marco's rubbing off on you."

"No, no. You twist everything up, Marco's friend."

"Oh, so it's back to that, is it? Carma, let me have your coat for a second. I have an idea."

"What are you going to do with it?" I took the coat and slipped it over Borgnine's shoulders and put his arms through the sleeves. Then I buttoned the coat up, and stood back to admire my handiwork. The image of a stuffed grizzly bear wearing a white polar bear coat was suffused with such irony, pathos, bathos, and tragedy, that I, there in my apartment at three o'clock in the afternoon on a cold winter's day in downtown Toronto at the absolute nadir of my life in front of my best friend's friend and in the midst of the ruins of a love gone, gone, gone away, had the best idea in history. No, really, I did.

"Your polar bear coat on my stuffed grizzly bear reminds me of the time that guy carrying the peanut butter collided with that other guy carrying the chocolate. I'm going to do an installation of animals dressed in the pelts of other species. What do you think?"

She sort of nodded and shook her head at the same time. She was right. Maybe art was the answer.

I got to work. Carma was gracious enough to lend me the coat as a gesture of a friend of a friend in need. Besides, she'd neglected to bring a gift this visit so she owed me. Borgnine looked spectacular in it, like a big NBA player on a roll. He was a bit butch, though. A leopard-skin pillbox hat immediately faggotized him, and the alligator purse, which I dangled from his limp wrist, completed the castration, as it was a good place for him to keep his balls. I was very pleased.

But I hadn't quite articulated my vision yet. I had to go deeper. Kate bought me a big white Belgian rabbit from the butcher. She had lovely features, with big pink eyes, but her complexion was wan. I knew that with the right makeup, I could bring out her luminous beauty. Of course I only used cosmetics that had been tested on rabbits, because I didn't want to irritate her eyes. At first she struggled, but once she saw herself all done up in the mirror, in a smart chinchilla stole, she was sold. I called her Goldie, after Goldie Hawn. She was a pleasant companion, and I must say, on the days she wore makeup, she was nicer. Whether that's a comment about women or rabbits, I don't know. That's best left to the philosophers.

But I still hadn't cracked that nut. I had to go deeper into myself. I got a fish, a largemouth bass, and placed him inside a large tank. He sunk to the bottom with a sigh, and his big bass lips curled down in sadness. He had the blues, so I called him Satchmo. I had to do something to cheer him up. I took a single, elegant strand of baby white pearls, which is really just dried oyster spit, and dipped them in the water. He looked up, swam toward them, and slipped them on. His demeanor changed instantly. In fact, I don't think I've ever seen a happier fish. I was getting there. I was really close.

Maybe the problem was that I was going after exotic animals, like rabbits and bass. What about something a little closer to home? I went over to my bag of animal parts and began rooting through them. A striped calico-cat tail caught my interest. At that moment, Kate walked in with her dog, a handsome rottweiler named Max. A lightbulb went off in my head. I dressed him up in a little leather vest and a leather cap. I got an instant erection, and so did Max, but we hid them from Kate as it would kill her to know that her dog was a fag. Masculinity was so important to her.

Then I took a photograph of Max looking over his shoulder with the calico cat's tail hanging out of his ass. When he saw himself in the mirror, he got so excited he spunked on the floor. I had done it! I had finally disgusted myself. I didn't realize it until that moment, that this is what I had been trying to do all along. I had broken on through to the other side. Finally, I could mend.

Life started to return to normal. Kate began dating this early lipstick lesbian, right out of *I Heard the Mermaids Singing*. Her name was Rona Gupta, a striking, fortyish East Indian woman. She was the curator of the ContempraART Gallery, and after seeing some of my Max pictures she became intrigued by what she called my work and which I called my LIFE.

"Your work really shows a fascinating multilevel relationship with the natural world, a love of nature yet tempered with rage toward the natural space. It challenges our concept of animals as lesser beings and calls into question our long domination of the 'lower' species."

"I know, and doesn't Goldie look pretty in that shade of blue?" I asked. She looked over at Goldie who was watching *Another World* on TV.

"She's obsessed with Erica Kane," I whispered to Rona.

"Why are you whispering?" she asked me.

"If she hears Erica's name she shits herself." I watched a brown marble roll across the floor.

"She heard!" I got up with a sigh and went for the broom. It seemed like all I did was follow Goldie around cleaning up her shit. Such a lazy little bitch. Why did I love her?

Rona said that my show would be huge, a wake-up call to the Toronto arts community. She described my work as William Wegman meets Helmut Newton. She said I'd be bigger than Warhol. It all made me nervous. One moment I was a model, the next I was a conceptual artist. There were so many facets to me. Would there ever be enough time in my life span to polish them all? I'd have to live to 190 to exhaust my full potential.

The show was to take place at her studio. Kate and I installed the installation. We placed Borgnine in the dead center on a huge granite pedestal. He towered above the room, glowering down in all his finery, and lit dramatically from above so as to minimize his double chin. To his left was Satchmo's tank, and to his right was a giant little girl's dollhouse. It was finely appointed with all the amenities. At the back of the gallery was a massive photo blow-up of "Max with a Cat's Tail up His Ass."

The day of the opening arrived. Rona advised me to brace myself for a tidal wave of attention. The first person to show up was a balding, twenty-something young white man wearing sandals, Indian pants, a hemp shirt, and some sort of African head garb. He appeared agitated, and came up to me with "Mission" written all over his face.

"Mr. Cole, I am here to protest your inappropriate use of the animal kingdom."

"And who might you be?"

"I am Bryden Happlecake. Your installation takes away the dignity of all animals."

"On the contrary, Mr. Happlecake, I am returning their dignity. I don't think I've ever seen a dignified fish before Satchmo." I gazed with fondness at the old bluesman. I had added a little sea horse stickpin to his chest and it looked darling.

"I am filled with revulsion at this display of man's inhumanity to man," he sputtered.

"Calm down, Bryden. These are animals."

"That rabbit has more humanity than you."

"That might be true. Goldie is a special rabbit." She was watching TV in her little pink dollhouse.

"She's graduated from the soaps to that new home shopping channel," I confided. "She's going to break me, you know. I hope she marries someone rich. And Jewish. Oh, well, we can only raise them, eh, Bryden? Then they're on their own. Well, I must be off. I've got to talk to my dealer."

"What kind of art dealer would peddle in obscenities like your work?"

"Not my art dealer. My drug dealer. I'm going to need to get wasted after this fiasco. Good day, Mr. Happlecake." I walked over to Rona who was attempting to bring people in off the street.

"Well, we haven't sold anything yet, but nobody buys at an opening, Buddy. They always come back the next day. I've taken a lot of phone numbers."

"But there's no one here."

"They're all coming later." She made the universal symbol for money and walked on. Suddenly a man walked in. He was

tall, whip thin, and dead white, with shiny blue-black hair and
an air of cruelty. He walked up to the photo of Max with the
cat tail up his ass and stared at it intently. I alerted Rona.

"Rona, go see if he's interested. I'm going to go over there
and get my credit card back from Goldie." She went up to him
and they spoke for a moment. Then he left and she walked
back over to me.

"Well, who was he? Anyone important?"

"Just some bum from New York named Mapplethorpe,"
she said dismissively. "Who was that bald man you were talking to earlier?"

"Some idiot going on about animal rights. What's next, gay
rights? Anyway, I'm going to step out for some air," I said.
This was so humiliating. I'd put my heart and soul on the line
and it had been stepped on. Not even Kate showed up. The
moment the last rivet went into Borgnine's pedestal, she was
out of there.

I pulled on my new caribou coat and went outside. It was
freezing, and starting to snow. Then I could see why no one
was coming in. Bryden Happlecake was standing in the front
of the building handing out flyers with a bunch of other losers.
I grabbed one of the flyers. It had a picture of a chimpanzee
with electrodes protruding from his head. There are other
ways to affix a hat, you know. Ever heard of bobby pins?
Anyway, the picture was a real downer and was scaring everyone away. I decided to make short work of Mr. Happlecake.

"Sir, you are ruining my parade. No one wants to look at a
chimp's bloody head except maybe another angry chimp.
None of the animals in my show are being harmed. In fact,
they're developing self-esteem. Before she met me, Goldie
couldn't even send food back at a restaurant. Satchmo was a
heroin addict. These animals owe me their lives. Can't you see
how I'm educating them? Of course, I'll agree with you, the
bear is a bit dim. Zero retention," I said, leaning deep into Mr.
Happlecake's personal space. "But he is nice to curl up with

on a cold winter's night, I'll tell you. And I'm not the only one who knows that. The other night, Marian Engel wouldn't stop calling. Eventually, I had to take the phone off the hook. What's next with you fanatics? Vegetarianism?"

"I myself am a vegan."

"Not a Trekkie, too!" I said, throwing my hands to the sky.

"Our organization believes no animal should be killed for any purpose, be it meat, fur, or scientific experimentation."

"What's your organization called?"

"We don't have a name yet."

"How pathetic. Everything has a name. Why don't you call yourself the pathetic empty tragic asswipes?" He seemed to be calculating something in his head as he listened to me.

"P-E-T-A. PETA!" He jumped up and grabbed one of the other losers. So once again, good reader, I somehow gave birth to another dreary modern phenomenon.

I went back inside and leaned disconsolately against my Borgnine. The dramatic lighting gave me a ghoulish appearance. I could see Rona in the corner on the phone. She gave me the universal symbol for money again. Goldie looked at me with *j'accuse* in her eyes. This was going to cost me another fur coat. Then I looked over at Satchmo. I could tell he was thinking of the needle and the damage done. This show had meant even more to them that it did to me, and I had let them down.

Then Kate stumbled in, stinking drunk, followed by of all people Ralph. And he wasn't alone. A tiny hand puppet of a boy trailed behind him. The boy had red hair, bad skin, and was skinny but with tits. I got dumped for this? Ralph walked up to me as though nothing had ever happened between us.

"Well, you've managed to write yourself back into this chapter," I spat out. "How could you ever leave your fabulous Sudbury?"

"Nonna wanted you to have this," he said, holding out a severed duck's foot. He pulled the nerve ending and it opened and closed. The thought of Nonna melted my heart. If only she had had a four-inch cock.

"Buddy, I'd like you to meet Mark," he said, presenting the boy.

"Nice to meet you," I said to him. "I hope you have a heart of steel. You're gonna need it. So where were you two tonight?" I said, switching gears.

Mark flinched. "We . . ." His voice trailed off. I just stared at him.

"Yes?" I encouraged.

". . . Ethiopian . . ."

"Uh-huh." I prompted.

". . . restaurant . . ."

"Oh, so you got to eat with your hands," I said. "That must have been nice for Ralph."

"I just wanted to come by, see your show, and I hope there's no hard feelings," said Ralph.

"I'm getting by. However, a lifetime of pain can't be wiped clean, like a blackboard or a dusty piano. Ralph, I know it must have been hard to contain a free-spirited creature like me. You tried, in your old-fashioned Italian way, to tie me down to the stove like your grandmother, but that isn't me. I think you just better go away and try to forget me. It's better for everyone."

"Are you trying to grow a beard?" asked Ralph.

"Mark," I said to the boy, "nice to meet you. And if you don't mind my saying so, I think your Ethiopian restaurant anecdote needs a little embellishing. Why don't you try a verb? Good night to you both." Ralph and his little friend slunk out the door. I turned and saw Kate puking her guts out into Satchmo's tank. I went over and put my arm around her.

"I'm sorry," she blubbered.

"That's okay," I told her. "I forgot to feed him today, anyway. Let's go home, girl. I've got to shave."

Caliguli,

Caligula

In this next section, you will be exposed to disturbing imagery and graphic depictions of wanton behaviour. Now, if you are the mythical under-seventeen-year-old addressed in the introduction, this is the time to put the book down, or at least turn on the night light. It gets very dark from here on in. And, if you've just raced ahead to the dirty parts like I told you not to, go back, you brat.

My goal is not to shock and horrify, but to tell the truth and if that truth shocks and horrifies, well, maybe you should get out more. This is my life. I stand by everything I've ever said or done, although I completely refute that last statement.

These scenes that you are about to read are not meant to be prurient, but rather educational, to alert all of us to the dangers of not knowing when to stop! I would also like to take this opportunity to acknowledge a certain someone whom I have been court-ordered not to include in this portrait of the gay *demimonde en crise*. Some stories are so juicy they're best left to a death bed confession, aren't they, Henry? Or should I say "H"?

Finally, in this section, everything takes place in a bleak

Bergmanesque winter. It was the winter that lasted close to three years. You'll understand soon enough.

With that said, I invite you now to enjoy the "wages of sin" section of *Buddy Babylon*.

Hello sodom, good night gomorrah

There came a day when all the Juicy Mango Jeans money ran out and I was forced to move out of Pierre's apartment, which had been my home for years. I took a one-bedroom apartment downtown in a giant high-rise in the gay ghetto affectionately known to the citizens as Vaseline Towers. I was also forced to get a real job. Yes, dear reader, I had to return to the working world. I became an esthetician at the Clinique counter at Holt Renfrew, Canada's most prestigious luxury department store. The money wasn't so good, but I got to wear a fetching smock and advise some of the country's richest women on how to look their best. If someone rubbed me the wrong way, I always gave them bad advice. I once told the seventy-something wife of a prominent politician, who made the mistake of calling me "Miss," that white lipstick and gold glitter eye shadow would look good on her. However, my plan backfired. She ended up finding herself, leaving her husband, and taking up Rollerblading. Even when I tried to do evil, I ended up doing good.

Though I hated my job, and romance had become something I watched actors pursue on TV, I was happy, because Marco was finally returning home after several years in Sweden. He had had an accident involving the Thor Saw and a volunteer at an industrial trade show. Luckily, every Swede was covered by healthcare, but Marco was still let go. He was returning to Canada on the 8:30 P.M. flight, so Carma Norma and I went to pick him up in her top-of-the-line Mercedes Benz. I was glad I was in a good car, as the roads were very icy. She was wearing something that looked like two tracksuits sewn together. As we waited for Marco to come through the arrivals gate, we chatted stiffly. It turned out that Marco wrote her far more often than me, and I was jealous. Maybe if I'd written back just once, but you can't undo the past. Too bad, because then I could go back and kill Bertolt Brecht. Suddenly, we heard a familiar voice pierce through the general hubbub. It was our pal.

"Carma!" shouted Marco, running toward her. Halfway there, he noticed me and changed his trajectory.

"Buddy!" Carma and I extended our arms like a finish line. He came within two feet of us, and in a quandary over which one to hug, embraced himself.

"I'm back!" he said exultantly. Then he walked up and slid an arm around each of us, pulling us together in a loving embrace.

"Ah, my best friends and compatriots. Well, how do I look?" The truth was, although still thin, he looked terrible. He had dyed his hair blond, which looked incredibly phony against his olive complexion.

"Your hair has gone Swedish," I said, trying to put the best spin on it.

"I know. Do you like it?"

"I love it," said Carma obsequiously. "You look so much younger."

I said nothing.

"I am younger," he said. "I've turned back the clock. I've discovered a new regime. Wolfsbane enemas. Buddy, you must try them. Makes the skin glow, as well as the added feature of keeping werewolves at bay."

"Well, it's really working. There's not a werewolf in sight. Let's go back to my place. My friend Kate's there, making dinner. She's dying to meet you."

When we arrived, Kate was by the stove, stirring a big pot. I made the introductions.

"I'm so pleased to finally meet you. I've heard so much about you," said Kate to Marco.

"Really? I've heard nothing about you. Buddy never writes, you know. But I'm sure everything I haven't heard is good."

"You must be hungry. I know what airplane food is like. I made a big pot of chili."

"I love chili, but I can't eat it. It doesn't agree with me. Gives me black water."

Marco made a beeline over to the bookshelves Kate had built for me. "Shoddy workmanship, Buddy. Who put them together? Out-of-work organ-grinder monkeys?"

Kate blanched. This wasn't going the way I had planned.

"By the way, where's the four-hundred-dollar chair?" Marco continued, striking oil once again.

"Um, it's touring the province on a train in an exhibit called 'Four-Hundred-Dollar Chairs Throughout Herstory,'" I told him. The truth was, I hated it and had put it in storage.

"Well, at least one of us is working. I always knew great things would come of that chair," he babbled. "By the way, how's Pornygirl or whatever her name is?"

"She's good."

"Excellent. I'm just going to freshen up after that economy-fare rodeo ride in the sky. I'll be out in a jiff," he said, disappearing into the bathroom with his black tote. I turned to Kate.

"Don't mind him, it's just jet lag."

"I'd love a bowl of your chili," said Carma.

"Yes. Me, too," I said. Though stung, Kate gave each of us a bowl, and I turned on the television. *The Wizard of Oz* was on. Dorothy was singing "Over the Rainbow," and we all fell under its spell. After about half an hour, Kate got up to use the facilities, but Marco was still inside. He said he would be out in a minute. Twenty minutes later, he still hadn't emerged. Finally, Kate had had enough and decided to go home to use her own bathroom. I knew she wouldn't be returning. Seconds later, Marco emerged looking refreshed.

"Where's that Kate fellow?"

"She went home."

"I have coke," said Carma. She held up a little plastic bag filled with cocaine.

"All the more for us," said Marco, grabbing the bag and dumping some on my black lacquer coffeetable.

"I do the honours," he said, pulling out a credit card. "After all, it's my birthday."

"No, it's not. You just returned from Sweden after being away for three years," I reminded him.

"Oh, yes. Well, I knew it was some sort of occasion," he said, taking a snort. "Ah, there's no place like home." Carma did her ration, and then handed me a rolled-up hundred-dollar bill. I hesitated because I knew that cocaine was not my friend, but the hundred dollars beckoned like a siren. Maybe I could palm the bill. After all, my finances were extremely tight at the time, and she sure wouldn't miss it. What was I thinking? Stealing from a friend of a friend. Shaking off the impulse, I accepted the line, and then handed back the bill. That was close.

Then we decided to go out on the town to the hot new nightclub, The Vatican, which was located in a former Catholic church that had gone out of business. I had become quite an habitué there recently. We took Carma's luxurious Mercedes and arrived at the church of sin. We went to the coat check, and found no line, which was odd, considering it was a Friday. I had to admit though, you did see a lot less people out and about now.

As soon as we entered the main room, Carma rushed off to

the washroom to powder her nose inside and out. Marco and I scrutinized the place. Laser lights swept a vast, empty dance floor as house music blasted from the speakers. Stained-glass windows of Christ and his posse were lit from behind with pulsating lights. At the front of the church, a DJ was set up on the altar. A huge neon cross blazed behind him. There were about twelve people dancing listlessly, and one old woman wearing white lipstick and gold glitter eye shadow whirling around on Rollerblades. It wasn't the same old woman, though. I guessed the trend was spreading.

"Where is everybody? It's like it's still a church," said Marco. "Buddy, is it true what they say? That AIDS has decimated our fair community? Sweden's so out of the loop. I don't know one person who has AIDS."

"Yes, it's true, Marco. Do you remember Andre, that really skinny guy who used to know every Broadway show tune at the Trax piano bar? Well, he got so skinny he just disappeared. And Little Johnny, the hairdresser from Victor's Salon? He's gone. Same with Dr. Paul. And his lover, remember David Dilley, he's gone too. Not dead, just gone. Let's face it, Marco. Since you left, half the people we used to know are dead. What are you drinking?"

"Under the circumstances, a triple Scotch. One for each brother lost."

"In that case, I'll bring you the bottle."

"You're okay, aren't you?" he asked, worry flaring in his face.

"Of course. I'm sure I'm fine. I mean, I've never really done anything that would give me cause for concern. Uh-huh, I feel good. Really un-AIDSy."

"Don't die on me." Marco looked at me with something approaching seriousness. I'd never seen it on him before and I had to admit, it gave him a certain James Brolin quality.

"I wouldn't die on my very best friend," I said. "Who would interpret you?"

"Thanks." We embraced. "Buddy, let this hug be a symbol of the newfound blend of friendship and concern we have for each other in every phase of our life-cycle circumstances, but especially this one, which is so distraught with difficulty."

"I love you, too," I said, interpreting. I went to the bar. The bartender, Steven, was a part-time drag queen and one of my bar buddies. The first time I met him he was in drag, and the next time he wasn't, and he got all bent out of shape because I didn't recognize him. That's one of the problems of gay life—having to know people in and out of drag. Twice the acquaintances but half the friends.

"Buddy, I haven't seen you in a whole day. Where have you been?"

"My friend Marco's back from Sweden. He's been gone for years, and I'm reacclimatizing him to our ways."

"He'll need shooters, then."

"So true. I'll have six Orgasms, a triple Scotch, one Brown Cow, and a vodka martini, straight up with an olive."

"Coming right up!" As he prepared the libations, I noticed that he was wearing rubber gloves. People really were getting paranoid. He chatted as he worked.

"By the way, I have a new drag character, Grabba Holdy. She's got red hair. She's totally different than my last drag character, Ofra Rack, who as you know was blond. That's probably why you didn't notice me that time."

"That must have been it. The only blond I recognize is the one in the mirror."

"Hey, Buddy, remember Uli, the leatherman who ran The Saunter On Inn?"

"Of course. He was the first person I met when I came to Toronto. How is the old dear?"

"He passed away yesterday."

"AIDS?" I asked.

"What else? He was only thirty." I was shocked. I couldn't

believe he was only thirty. Steven handed me a tray of drinks. I realized I was flat broke.

"Can I put it on my tab?" I asked.

"Okay," he said a little reluctantly.

"By the way, what is my tab now?"

"Four hundred dollars."

"Do you like chairs?" Minutes later, I had arranged to settle my bill. I brought back the drinks to the gang. Carma and Marco were deep in thought. But unfortunately, they were speaking them aloud. I listened to them for a few minutes while they nattered on about the miracle of tea tree oil, completely oblivious to me. Finally Marco noticed me standing there.

"Ah, thank you, Buddy. Beverage for the brain."

"Marco, did you know that Uli died?"

"Buddy, stop with the death march already. I'm back. I'm blond. Good times ahead." Marco held his shooter aloft. Carma did the same. I sadly raised my arm.

"I've never had an Orgasm before," she said. So that was her problem.

"To us. Survivors! May we continue to survive at all costs," I said.

"Buddy, that's a little morbid," chastised Marco. "How about a toast to Linda Evangelista, Canada's greatest supermodel of all time?"

"I love her," said Carma. "Did you see that spread in *Vogue* where she has red hair and is all dressed in tartan in front of a Scottish castle?"

"Life-changing," said Marco. "To Linda!" We downed our drinks.

"I feel like dancing," I said, and rushed to the floor. The music hit me and I began to spin. I spun and spun and spun for a very long time until finally Marco came up to me.

"We want to go," he said.

"Just one more spin, please?" I spun one more time,

slipped, and fell on my face. I could feel my tooth pierce my lip and I tasted blood. I picked myself up and looked at Marco.

"Buddy, where's your gay equilibrium?"

"I guess I spun too much. I'm okay. Let's go to another place."

"That's what I said before," he bitched. "This wouldn't have happened if you'd listened to me the first time. How the hell you got along without me when I was away, I'll never understand." Back at the table, Carma was nervously shredding the paper tablecloth with nail clippers.

"Look what I did," she said, holding her handiwork aloft. I could tell Carma was hitting the slopes a little too often. The truth be told, I myself was drinking a little more than usual. But I knew that as long as I stayed away from cocaine, I was fine. Still, it was hard to resist, because now it seemed to be around all the time. I knew I was okay, though. After all, I had only done one line, although I couldn't help wondering how much Carma had. I suggested we repair to one of my favourite dance clubs, Everybody, and they were all for it. It was called Everybody because eventually everybody ended up there. We piled into Carma's car and drove to the club. Everybody was atop a clothing store. We walked up a long flight of metal stairs and at the top were greeted by a burly black doorman. It was my friend, Radisson. He didn't seem quite as burly as usual. My heart clenched.

"Hey, beautiful," he said as he moved in to kiss me on the lips. Without even thinking, I turned my head away and presented my cheek. I tossed it off as continental rather than paranoid.

"How you doing, Radisson?" I pronounced his name the French way. He liked that. His family came from St. Croix in the Caribbean.

"I'm okay. Are you going to be at the Vatican on the fourteenth? There's going to be a huge fund-raiser for AIDS."

"Really? I thought AIDS was doing just fine on its own. I'm

the one who needs a fund-raiser." We both laughed, and he used it as an opportunity to pull me close. Radisson and I had slept together once, but it didn't work out. Cornygirl didn't like him. But he still burned a candle for me.

"Gimee a call," he said.

"I will," I lied. We went inside. The joint was jumping. Lots of fags and black women.

"Well, there's nobody here," said Marco. "Let's do a line." We raced off to the ladies' room, crowded into a stall, and did a line each. I realize that a few pages ago I said that I knew that coke was bad for me but this was a special occasion. Marco and I had a lot of catching up to do. Therefore we needed to talk really fast. Marco wasn't interested in nostalgia though, as he and Carma were engaged in a fascinating conversation about beta-carotene as the first line of defense against cancer. I left them and returned to the dance floor. I was standing by the bar waiting for a good song when I noticed a chubby sad guy standing in front of me with a look of resignation on his face.

"Sorry, am I blocking your way?" I asked.

"It's okay, I can wait," he mumbled passively.

"So, you're just going to wait there until I move? What if I never move? What if I decide that this is the perfect place for me to spend the rest of my life? Are you going to move then, or are we both just going to stand here forever, locked in a battle of wills, until Judgment Day?"

"What?" he said.

"I'm sorry. I'm on truth mode tonight," I said. "You look like you just found out that people were executed for being fat. Smile for me, Tubby. That's your name, isn't it? If it's not, that's what you should call yourself. Reclaim the word from bathtub manufacturers." He seemed troubled, but forced a smile. He suddenly looked cute.

"There, isn't that better? Do you know that actually making a smile, even a fake one, forces endorphins into your face, which in turn fills your heart with happiness?"

"Thanks. I'll remember that the next time some guy passes me over for someone who looks like you."

"With that attitude, what do you expect?" I said. He pouted.

"I want you to do something for me, Tubby. I want you to take off your shirt."

"No. They'll laugh at me for not being thin and blond."

"Fuck them. They're on the way out. Trust me."

"But I'm fat."

"I'm tired of your excuses. They're flabby, Tubby." I reached over and ripped off his XXL, shapeless black T-shirt. He tried to cover his breasts like an actress playing a south seas maiden in a Hollywood movie.

"Now, get out there and shake those hairy tits. The world awaits." Then I grabbed his sad moon face and spun him around onto the dance floor. He landed right in the middle of a group of gyrating, zaftig black girls. At first he danced cautiously to the thumping house music, afraid to shake his soft white belly. It was going to take more than a pep talk. I went up to the DJ and made a request—"The Twist" by Chubby Checker. Immediately all the black women started to twist with abandon. Tubby just stood there awkwardly, like a little boy who had wandered into a herd of antelope. Then two of the women flanked him and started to bump him with their hips. In an effort to avoid them, he began to twist himself. But it still wasn't happening. Thinking fast, I raced onto the dance floor and shoved my little brown bottle of poppers under his nose. He took a sniff, and soon he was shaking it like Aretha.

Who would have guessed that fatties need to sweat to the oldies? Years later, Richard Simmons stole my idea and I've never seen a red cent. I met Richard once, on a famous daytime talk show. We were both guests on an episode entitled "Effeminate Men and the Fat Women Who Love Them." After the show, he gushed inordinately but I managed to hold off his enthusiasm with an energy bar.

People were drawn to Tubby's sexual awakening on the dance floor. Soon, a young, thin blond guy was staring at him with obvious lust. I could sense something happening, some sort of new sexual category of attractiveness being born. Tubby finished dancing and came up to me. He looked incandescent.

"Wow, that was great. That blond guy over there is staring at me."

"Go for it. You know, you're really sexy. You remind me of my bear."

"I kind of feel like a bear," he growled, and ran off to his blondezvous. And with that, I gave birth to the Bear Movement. My missionary work was done. Time for some R'n'R.

I spotted a beautiful black guy, dressed very collegiately and wearing glasses, standing by himself at the back of the club. He looked bored. Our eyes met, and there was an instant connection. Both of us resisted the impulse to be the first to go to the other. And then I gave in. I didn't want to blow this opportunity. Well, actually, I did.

"You look as excited as someone waiting for a bus to Brampton," I said to him.

"I *am* from Brampton," he said.

"Oh, that's hilarious. I'm from Brampton, too," I said, seized by a sudden desire to fib.

"You are? What school did you go to?"

"The big one," I hazarded.

"You mean, Centennial?"

"That's the one."

"That was my high school. What year did you graduate?"

"The same year as the teacher's strike," I said, bluffing.

"That was my year. I think I know you. You were the quarterback of the football team," he said excitedly. This was beyond my wildest dreams. I went for it.

"Remember this?" I said, putting my arm back in a throwing position and faking a toss.

"Yes, yes," he cried, remembering somebody else's football glory.

"That's what helped us defeat— Do you remember what school? See if you know it."

"T. L. Kennedy!" he said, jumping up. "I remember you! You ended our twenty-six-year losing streak!"

"That's right. And, with a sprained wrist."

"I don't remember that."

"I kept it quiet. I didn't want anyone's pity. Did you play ball at all?"

"No, my mother wouldn't let me," he said. "Hey, do you remember me?"

"Yes. I have a distinct memory of you drinking water from a fountain in the hall."

"I used to do that."

"Oh, the good old days, eh? If only we knew then what we know about each other now."

He took my hand and led me through the club to the back room. We pushed our way past many groping, grunting men, and found a space in the back. He had a beautiful cock. He really should have played football. He liked mine, too. Apparently, I was quarterback size. After blowing each other for a while, we both came, thanked each other, and walked out. I told him to say hello to the old gang. Then he patted me on the ass.

"Wow. I finally had Randy Gerber," he said. "See ya, Randy." I slipped into the washroom to clean up. When I looked in the mirror, I gasped in shock. The wound on my lip stood out in bas-relief. I had totally forgotten about it. I tasted pre-cum where, only an hour earlier, the taste of blood had been. I couldn't believe my carelessness. Ever since the plague had begun, I had been so rigorous in my observance of safe sex. You might even say, fanatical. At one time I'd even given up phone sex. But recently I'd begun to relax my standards. They said you couldn't get AIDS from oral sex. However, *they* never saw me give head. It must have been because of Marco's return. I decided that if I tested positive I'd blame him. I went to find the bastard.

I found him and Carma in a back corner engaged in a furious debate over the benefits of exfoliation. I told Marco that his new blond hair against his olive complexion somehow made him look East Indian whereupon he broke down crying. He then promised me he would change it the next day. What a victory! I had finally found a way to put my pettiness and Marco's racism to good use.

The 120 days
of joey

One Tuesday, Marco and I rushed off to the Vatican. When we got there, we were pleasantly surprised to find that the place was packed. Something was up. Marco grabbed a beer, I ordered a martini, and we started circulating. The lights came up onstage and out walked Steven as his new drag character, Grabba Holdy. He was wearing the same tawdry Bob Fosse rip-off he always wore but this time he had red hair. I have to honestly say, Grabba still didn't grab me. She gripped the mike and spoke. But it wasn't on, so no one could hear her. Everyone kept talking. Suddenly, the mike came on really loud and her voice kicked everyone in the head.

"—so enjoy the contest!" she yelled, feedback filling the smoky air.

"What contest?" someone yelled back.

"Miss Tuesday Night. I just told you." The mike had gone dead again.

The same person yelled back, "The mike wasn't on, you drunk hag."

"Yeah, I'll bet you got a little one," she shot back, lamely.

"Oh, yeah?" the guy said. He undid his button fly and fished out an enormous cock. "You call this little?" Everyone cheered. Wit had won again. Grabba said something, but the microphone had gone dead once more, so we will never know how brilliant her retort might have been. The mike came back on.

"The idea is to interpret the concept of Tuesday. The first contestant is George." Grabba motioned to the side of the stage, and just stood there, stealing focus. George came out naked wearing only a sandwich board with a calendar on it. All the Tuesdays were circled, and his cock and balls poked through the last Tuesday of the month. On his penis was written DJ HARRY BARRIS EVERY TUESDAY AT THE VATICAN. It was so big you could read every word clearly. I turned to Marco.

"That George guy is the owner Julius's boyfriend. He's just using the contest to advertise another event."

"Sickening," he responded automatically, hypnotized by the cock. "What were you saying?"

"Our next contestant is this year's emperor of the Royal Monarchist League," said Grabba. "Please welcome Jeremy Lunenberg as Tuesday's Child, Full of Grace." Out walked a pale, haunted-looking man, about forty, with dark circles under his eyes like in those big-eyed waif pictures. He was dressed like Pierrot except for his emperor's sash. He stood there awkwardly by the calendar guy.

"Looks more like Wednesday's child, full of woe," I whispered to Marco.

"I know. Absolutely no basket."

"Smile! It's free!" came a voice from the crowd. It was that big, obnoxious guy again. Grabba's mike went dead once again, and I took the opportunity to investigate Mr. Belligerent. He was a handsome, muscular guy, with dark blond hair and a big, ready grin. He was obviously completely plastered, and gave off an air of blistering sexual energy. One could almost see his brain moving, struggling to come up with more quips. Suddenly, I saw an idea form on his face.

"Take it off!" he yelled. I laughed. I liked this guy. The

microphone came back on, and Grabba once again tried to win back the attention of the room, which continued talking.

"Our third contestant is from Hamilton, but don't hold that against her. Here's Steeltown's own Tuesday Welder." A skinny drag queen wearing a welder's mask and carrying a blowtorch stode out onstage to the strains of S'Express's "Suck Me Off" with guest vocalist Karen Finley. She wore a little, sixties-style miniskirt and stood at the front of the stage with her legs spread. She pulled back the mask and revealed a face exactly like Tuesday Weld in *Pretty Poison.* And even though I hate drag, I had to approve. She pulled her blowtorch up like a gun. Blue flame shot out the end. She opened her little white purse and pulled out a length of copper pipe, held it up to the blowtorch, heated it till it was red hot, and then, like a strongman, bent the pipe as everybody screamed. Even the sexy boor was cheering. It was no contest.

The three contestants huddled at the side of the stage and Grabba consulted with the celebrity judges. They were Julius, the owner of the bar, a big, handsome, aging boy toy; another drag queen called Hedda Hair, the biggest mess since Craig Russell; and Peter Pounces, the editor of Toronto's only gay newspaper, *X-Crete,* a towering mass of easily offended flesh. Grabba grabbed back the stage from the unruly crowd and announced the winner.

"The winner of the Miss Tuesday contest is . . . George!" There was mixed applause and scattered *boos.* I was outraged and turned to Marco.

"That's disgusting. It's fixed. He just won because he's the owner's boyfriend."

"Yes, but he did show his cock," Marco pointed out. The worst part was, Julius had a huge cock, too. I don't think it's right when a relationship takes two big ones out of circulation. That's why I'm not a size queen. The lights dimmed and the people onstage wandered off haphazardly. Another glorious end to a well-orchestrated drag show. The music resumed.

People began to dance, and the club returned to normal. I saw Grabba Holdy moving through the crowd toward me.

"Hi, Grabba," I said. "Great show."

"It's Steven," he said in his normal, gay male voice.

"But you're dressed as Grabba."

"Yeah, but I'm talking as Steven."

"I see." I didn't.

"Anyway, thanks for the four-hundred-dollar chair, Buddy. I love it. It's my good-luck charm. Oh, I gotta go. I got a show at the 501 later." He suddenly threw his head back dramatically and flung his arms to the sky. "Ta-ta, toenails. See you in your dreams."

"Good-bye, Steven," I said.

"It's Grabba!" he yelled, possessed, and swept off. Marco turned to me with fury on his face.

"Did I hear something about a four-hundred-dollar chair, Buddy?"

"Yes. Well, it returned from the train tour last week—I forgot to tell you, sorry—and it was a huge hit. Anyway, Grabba saw the chair on its stop in Oshawa and fell in love with it. When she found out I was the actual owner, she asked if she could buy it, and under the circumstances, I didn't have the heart to say no." I dropped my voice. "She's, um, sick, you know. She's got it."

"I had no idea," said Marco seriously.

"Yes, very sad. But apparently the chair is the only thing keeping her alive, as you just overheard."

"My God, Buddy. That chair's a goddamn miracle worker. Makes you believe in God. They should canonize it. Saint Chair!" We turned our attention back to the dance floor. Marco and I watched as the boor took off his shirt and began to dance, lost in his own body.

"What a noble savage," I said, captivated.

"A little rough around the edges, but still, a blond," agreed

Marco. The guy stopped and saw us looking at him. He smiled and walked over.

"That contest was pretty lame, eh?" he said.

"I couldn't believe that guy won," I said.

"My name's Joey," he replied. "You guys want to smoke a joint?" We wandered out onto an outdoor deck. It was freezing. Joey still had his shirt off. Judging by his nipples, I'd have to say it was about forty below. I squeezed them playfully.

"Hello, how do you do?" I said to each one. Joey laughed and lit a big fat spliff. He passed it around and we smoked it, Canadian-style—cursing the cold and coughing.

"You guys aren't drag queens, are you? Because I hate drag queens," he said.

"We're just queens," I replied. Joey looked around and saw a hot guy standing nearby. His eyes widened with mischief. "You guys finish that joint. I'm taking it easy tonight. I did a hit of MDA and a little coke, so I figure I'm fine for now. Maybe later when I come down off the blow, and I need to take the edge off, I'll drop a 'lude, unless the M has kicked in by then, in which case I'll be fine."

"A night off is good. It gives you time to take stock," I said.

"I'm gonna check that guy out," said Joey. He approached his prey. Without a word, the guy fell to his knees and began to blow Joey. We watched them with rapt attention, as if it was nature documentary footage of a python swallowing a rabbit. After the deed was done, Joey ambled back to us, his mouth slack like a lion after a kill. I knew with this guy I'd be making a lot of animal metaphors.

We went inside and got drinks. A television monitor above the bar was playing the 1970s classic *The Boys in the Band*. It was the first time in years I'd seen anything but porn in a gay bar. Now I have nothing against porn but I just don't think gay men need to be reminded of sex. Marco looked at the TV and shuddered.

"Where's the cock?" he said. I snapped.

"Does everything have to have cock with you? When you saw the 'Mona Lisa,' did you say, 'Where's the cock?' "

"No, Buddy. Actually what I said was, 'It's so small.' "

"My God, you're even a size queen about paintings."

There was an uncomfortable silence. This kind of thing had been happening a lot lately. I knew it was from the coke, and resolved to stop. Then Joey broke the tension by pointing out some other fags we could take our self-loathing out on, Todd Taylor-Fenski and David Fenski-Taylor, a pair of beautiful bodybuilder lovers who had gotten married and written a book. They were holding hands and talking quietly, lost in each other's gorgeousness.

"They're monogamous, you know," I began. "Five years. Todd told me breathlessly about it the first time I met him. Apparently, it *realllllly* works for them. Now, I have nothing against monogamy. But trust me, with most fags, it's not cheating unless you're actually playing cards."

"That's for sure," said Joey. "You see the one on the right? I fucked him." I was shocked. If you couldn't believe in identical gay lovers, what could you believe in? Then everyone wanted to go to the Baths but I told them that I was tired and was just going to go home to do a masque. The truth was, I was engulfed in AIDS paranoia, which had continued ever since the cut-lip incident. Marco seemed to know what I was thinking.

"Buddy, all safety considerations aside, just don't do anything I wouldn't do."

"You mean dye my hair an unflattering colour?"

"Look, it's gone. Can't you let it rest?" shrieked Marco in a complete overreaction.

"I've got blow," said Joey, once again to the rescue. That was all I needed. My resolve dissolved. I'll quit tomorrow, I said to myself, even if tomorrow was probably two weeks away. As for the growing tension with Marco, it disappeared the instant we did a line.

We soon found ourselves at the Parthenon Steam Club for Men. Joey and Marco quickly got lockers and went in. I lingered by the door, intrigued by the tender youth sitting behind the barred window. He was barely out of his teens, fair-skinned, with sandy brown hair, blue eyes, a lanky build, and full red lips. Innocence personified. Of course he was working in a bathhouse but that didn't really mean anything in gay terms. For many gay men, working in a bathhouse comes right after having a paper route.

"Aren't you Buddy Cole?" he asked.

"How do you know my name?"

"Everyone knows you. You're a legend."

"That's flattering but I'm too young to be a legend. Though it is gratifying to know that the tales of my exploits have reached even these parts."

"You bet! People are still talking about the night you drank that lesbian softball team under the table." Not exactly the legend I'd had in mind.

"Yes, I do lead a fascinating life."

"I see you at the Vatican all the time, you know."

"I'm in training."

"I always thought you were handsome." I had never been called handsome before. Gorgeous, stunning, charismatic, luminous, breathtaking, and statuesque, but never handsome. He continued. "But I was too shy to come up."

"Well, don't be. Next time come up and buy me a drink."

"I will." We looked at each other for a long time and then he let me in for free. I toddled off to my room, feeling like a teenager.

My room was the size of a large bathtub. The bed was a narrow plank with a thin, flat mattress upon it. It was covered by a sheet that was one washing away from a rag. There was a locker, and a small light with a dimmer switch. I immediately turned it down, creating the proper romantic mood. Then I took the rest of my clothes off, tied the towel around my head, and ventured forth. I attracted a lot of attention as I walked down the dark hallway. Literally everybody stared at me. I couldn't tell if it was my headdress or my swinging member. I had never felt so in control, my yin and yang perfectly balanced. After wandering a while through a maze of hallways, I came across Joey taking a shower. He noticed me and began to laugh hysterically.

"You look like the Sheikh of Arabia," he said.

"Exactly. And who wouldn't want to fuck the Sheikh of Arabia? Looks, and money, too." I took off my headdress and stepped into the shower stall. I noticed Joey checking me out. Not because he was interested, but because he wanted to know what I had. I could tell he was impressed. He was that type.

"Have you seen Marco?" I said, soaping up.

"Yeah. He was in the middle of a big scene in the porn room."

"He loves his porn."

"I never watch porn. When I'm horny, I just have sex," said Joey.

"What about when you masturbate?"

"I haven't jerked off in years. No need." I was astonished. To some of you, dear readers, I may appear as a slut, but next to someone like Joey, I'm practically a prude. Believe me, I love sex, but I can go for months without it. As long as I have my blue movies, I'm happy. And it's true that over the years I've watched everything imaginable that two to twelve men can do to one another. The difference between me and Joey was, he'd actually done it all. We both got out of the shower and toweled off. I put my headdress back on and flounced away. I noticed the boy from the front desk changing the sheets in a room, so I poked my head in.

"Can I help?" I asked, as he struggled with a sheet.

"No, I'm okay."

"Please. I grew up on a submarine. I know all about changing little beds." Without thinking, I entered the room and tucked the sheet under the mattress. He looked alarmed when he saw my nakedness.

"Am I making you uncomfortable?" I asked.

"No, but you're supposed to wear the towel around your waist, you know." Without a word, I took it off and tied it properly.

"There, now I've got my mystery back." He giggled. I hadn't heard anyone giggle in years.

"Well, I have to go find my friends. See ya," I said, and skipped off. I wanted to take this slowly as he was so young, and besides, I knew I was still too high on coke to do much.

I went to the sauna and peeked in. It was filled with Oriental men. No one was doing anything so I took a seat in the middle of the group. The guy beside me was cute and seemed interested. Our legs rubbed against each other. His hand crept under my towel and touched my thigh. I did the same to him. Then I leaned in and kissed him. His hand came up and gently touched my nipple. Soon our tongues were exploring each other's mouths. All of a sudden, every guy in the sauna was on me, each part of my body being fondled. It was too much attention, even for a model. I pushed them all away and fled the sauna. Marco happened to be passing by and noticed my distress.

"Buddy, what happened?"

"I was just swarmed by a group of super-horny Oriental men."

"Ah, yes, the fabled mosquito attack? It's happened to me many times."

"What would you call it if you got swarmed by a group of black men?"

"That would be a gang rape."

"And a group of white men?"

"An orgy."

"Marco, we should have been in Vaudeville." I left him and wandered around amusing myself for a few hours while I came down from the coke. I suddenly smelled the scent of laundry and was overwhelmed by images of Maman and that glorious pile of miners' lingerie. I followed the trail. It led to the only brightly lit room in the labyrinth of lust. I peeked inside, and saw the boy folding sheets and placing them on a shelf beside a giant dryer.

"At least you don't have to worry about separating whites and colours," I said, entering. He looked up, startled.

"Hey, dude."

"My mother used to take in laundry when we were poor," I told him, moving closer. "I used to help her. It was the only time we had to talk. The smell of laundry makes me feel safe."

"Yeah, I know what you mean. I just love to bury my face in clean sheets."

"Who said anything about clean laundry?" I had been moving in on him, and was now standing very close, both of us resting our backs against the huge dryer, which hummed and rattled. I noticed he was excited. My eyes feasted on his enthusiastic tumescence.

"It's because I'm standing next to the dryer," he said coyly, noticing.

"Me, too," I said, feeling stirrings down below signaling that I was finally coming down from the coke.

"Your towel looks dirty," he said, looking up like a shy fawn through thick eyelashes.

"It's filthy," I said, pulling it off slowly and handing it to him. He silently removed his pants and T-shirt and then stood there awkwardly in his gleaming white cheap underwear and running shoes. He leaned back against the spinning dryer and his whole body began to vibrate like a bee. A grin only seen on hustlers and angels split his face. The waiting was over. I leaned in and kissed him. My lips began to vibrate, too, and the tickling made me burst out laughing. He started to giggle and I fell upon him like a siren on a sailor. By the time we finished, I'd been cleansed. I always felt so much better after doing the laundry. Later that morning, while lying in bed clutching the memory in one arm and Cornygirl in the other, I realized that I hadn't even gotten his name.

My eighth birthday

I woke up one morning to a gruesome hangover and someone banging on the door. Reluctantly, I got up, shuffled over, and opened it with great difficulty. It was Kate, holding a brightly wrapped package and a bottle of Golden Wedding.

"You look like shit. You are doing way too much coke, you know," she admonished me.

"Keep your nose out of my nose's business. Anyway, you're one to talk, Miss Golden Wedding."

"I never missed a day of work because of my drinking."

"Well, it's easy when you're a location scout. You make your own hours, and besides, everybody's drunk on set. I have to be at that badly lit Clinique counter every morning at ten o'clock five days a week. All I'm saying is, I have a shitty job! Come in."

"You know it's eleven o'clock, don't you?"

"In the morning?" I asked.

"No, at night. Jesus, what's wrong with you?" I realized that I'd slept for twenty-two hours. Well, I must have really needed it.

"Anyway, happy birthday," she said.

"I totally forgot it was my birthday."

"I'm not surprised. You haven't answered your phone in two days. This place is a mess. It looks like a dirty hurricane passed through it."

I looked around at my apartment. Magazines, takeout detritus, and clothes lay everywhere in thick piles, oftentimes obscuring the furniture. I suddenly realized that all the walls of the apartment had been painted aquamarine blue. I had no recollection of doing it but had to admit that it looked stunning.

"How old are you anyway?" she asked.

"Seven," I lied. I was actually eight. That was the beauty of being born in a leap year. When you lied about one year, you actually took four off. "I'm old. That's over the hill in gay life."

"Not for dykes," she said.

"Yeah, but you girls like them old. We gay men don't become wise when we age, m'dear. We become 'trolls.' "

"Come on, troll. Make me some coffee." She grabbed my elbow and steered me into the kitchen where I banged about. I couldn't find a filter, but I did find a fairly clean pair of underwear on the counter. When I presented Kate with her coffee, she smacked her lips with satisfaction. This is the closest she'll ever get to a man's crotch, I thought. I hoped she wouldn't return the favour one day by making me herbal tea with her panties.

"I got you something," she said, handing me the brightly wrapped box. I tore off the wrapping paper to reveal a book called *1001 Excuses for Missing Work*.

"Very funny. But the truth is I never miss work. I'm just always late. Granted, sometimes, I'm eight hours late."

There was another knock at the door. It was Marco and Carma Norma, in huge winter coats and weighed down with gift boxes. They pushed their way inside.

"Happy birthday!" sang Marco. "All this bounty for you, my very best friend in the entire world—except for Carma—

who stood by me through thick and thin—hello, Kate—and even thinner."

"We brought gifts," said Carma. "Look. Gifts. Where should I put the gifts?"

"Just put them on the—" My black lacquer table had disappeared under a pile of junk. "Just hand them to me. I'll open them standing up." The first box contained a tiny Oscar engraved with the words ACADEMY AWARD FOR BEST FRIEND.

"Look, it's a little Academy Award," said Carma.

"Make a speech," urged Marco.

"I want to thank the element bronze for allowing itself to be poured into the shape of such a wonderful award." Everyone applauded. The second gift was a beautifully framed Polaroid of me performing fellatio.

"Oh, my God. Where was this taken?" I said with feigned embarrassment.

"At the Kennel, where else?" said Marco. The Kennel was our new hangout since the Vatican had closed. It had the same manager, Julius. We had sort of become friends, but mostly just because I was there all the time.

"Buddy, look what I noticed," said Marco excitedly. "Judging by the photo evidence, it seems that you uncross your eyes when there's a cock in your mouth." Sure enough, it was true. Maybe I should just start smoking cigars.

"Look, Kate," I said, showing her the picture. She barely looked at it.

"They got your good side," she sneered.

"Buddy, what happened to you the other night?" asked Marco. "The last I saw you, you were disappearing into the backroom at the Kennel with that professional wrestler. Got any bruises to prove it?"

"Just emotional ones."

"Hi. We've never met," said Carma turning to Kate.

"Yes, we have," Kate scowled.

"Of course," she stammered apologetically. "You're the scout leader."

"Location scout," Kate overpronounced.

"This is from me," Carma said, handing me another box. I tore into the wrapping to reveal a box of Carma Norma Bum Pads for Men. It was the same gift she gave everyone.

"How thoughtful, Carma," I said. "I myself am sufficiently upholstered, but you never know when I might want a huge ass. Maybe one day I'll find myself in Africa, with a bunch of Hottentots, and I'll want to impress them. One never knows."

"Or maybe you can give them to Kate," Marco said, turning on her. "Perhaps she can use them to fill out that impoverished bosom of hers." I laughed. Kate glared at me.

"What?" I asked her. "Do you want a line, or what?"

"You know, Buddy, you and your friends are losers," she announced, abruptly getting up. "You used to be funny and now you're just a coke hag." She left, slamming the door behind her. She must have been angry. It was the first time she had ever called me by my real name.

"Well, what was that all about?" asked Marco. "She *is* flat."

"That's sad," said Carma. "I have a gram. Want a line, Marco's friend?" I hesitated. I knew I shouldn't. But what the hell. It was my birthday.

I decided that since I was eight, I would dress as a little boy. And since I was apparently into some sort of blue period, I decided to go as Gainsborough's "Blue Boy."

I got dressed and we headed off to the Kennel Club. When we arrived, there was a long line of blue-lipped fags shivering in the cold, waiting to get in. We sashayed right past them. I've never been one for waiting in lines. The only time I ever did so was when I slept overnight at Ticketmaster to be the first in line to buy tickets for Cleo Laine featuring John Dankworth. I would only go that far for a five-octave range. Or maybe it was the word "master" in Ticketmaster.

Radisson was at the door that night. He looked even thinner than the last time I had seen him.

"Radisson, you look fab-u-lous!" I overreacted.

"You look like a meal for a Flemish pedophile," he said, giving me a wet kiss. "Happy birthday, girl."

"Thanks. I hope there's many more. Not that I mean anything by that. Anyway, I really need a drink. See you later, doll." I realized that I had never called anyone "doll" before. What was wrong with me? The minute I was out of his eyeshot, I wiped my mouth.

Inside, the place was jumping. There were shirtless men everywhere. I noticed that many of them seemed unnaturally muscular. I also noticed that the dog cages which lined the long narrow room were full. Each one held a sexy canine like a Doberman, a pit bull, a Labrador, or a rottweiler. I noticed Max in one, and he wagged his two tails at me. At the end of the room, it widened into a small stage area with a tiny dance floor in front. The stage was adorned with a huge banner saying HAPPY BIRTHDAY, BUDDY! Oh, my God, it was a party for me! Marco told me that this was Julius's way of thanking me for all the alcohol I had consumed at his establishments. All I had to do was make a speech, and drinks were on the house. Julius was suddenly beside me.

"Happy birthday, biggest customer. Come up when you're ready, although we need the dance floor in twenty minutes," he said and kissed me. I made my way toward the stage, with Marco and Carma in tow. The first person I saw was Joey, talking to two guys at the bar. He was showing them a scar below his bikini line.

"Birthday boy! What are you wearing? Pyjamas?" He gave me a big hug. I could smell his fresh-from-a-workout perspiration. He whispered in my ear, "I got something special for you."

"Animal, vegetable, or chemical?" I asked.

"All three," he said, handing me a translucent blue blob the size of a grape. It danced in my palm like a Mexican jumping bean.

"What is it?"

"I got it from a biker I did in a rest stop. He said they're called No Tomorrows."

"No time like now for a No Tomorrow," I said, taking the blob and swallowing it. It wriggled down my throat like a worm and you know, I can't say I didn't like it.

"Well, I must circulate. See you after the ceremony." I moved on. The next person I bumped into was Donal, a strikingly well-preserved man in his sixties with a fading British accent. He was fun to drink with, and always had some dish.

"Ah, Gainsborough's Blue Boy. Happy birthday! Yum yum, give me some," he said, grabbing my nipples. "I don't know if you heard about what happened at 'Last Tango in Paris Night' at the Condor last week, but boy, did the place ever get slutty. I guess that's what happens when you add a tub of butter to a roomful of inebriated homosexuals. Anyway, you should come next Saturday. It's going to be Doctor's Waiting Room Night. They're going to scatter ancient copies of *Redbook*, *Chatelaine*, and *Reader's Digest* on the bar, and a bunch of drag queens dressed up like nurses are going to walk around taking temperatures. At the end of the night, there's going to be a draw where the winner gets a free rectal examination onstage from Toronto's finest colon specialist, Dr. Sariq Khana."

"The man's a wizard with hemorrhoids." What was it with theme nights in gay life? I guess it's because our existence is so chaotic, we need themes to hold on to. They're the large print version of the Book of Life. Fags and people. Will I ever really understand why we're so different? Then I bumped into Tubby. He was wearing boots, jeans, and a leather vest so that his belly hung out. I could see that he'd gained a few pounds, but it looked good on him.

"I heard it was your birthday tonight, so I wanted to come and give you my best and introduce you to Bill. He knows all about you." Tubby motioned to the tall man standing behind him. He had thick metal hoops through his ears and a tusk through his nose. He looked blankly at me.

"I branded him," said Tubby, beaming.

"I hope you saved the receipt. After all, you only used it once. You can return it and get your money back," I said, moving on grandly. When I looked back, Bill was giving Tubby a boost into a sling. Ain't love grand?

I saw someone approaching with obvious Kaposi's Sarcoma on his face. He was smiling at me, and though he looked familiar, I couldn't place him. So, inspired by Princess Diana's recent visit to Casey House, Toronto's AIDS hospice, I extended my arms and asked him where he was from.

"It's me, Buddy. Ralph." It didn't register immediately because he didn't have a beard anymore. My inner Diana started slashing her wrists and throwing herself down the stairs.

"You've shaved your beard. I didn't recognize you. But that's the only reason."

"It looks bad, doesn't it?"

"No, not at all. It just looks like you had a bad spill."

"I tested positive two years ago."

"And we broke up four years ago. Not that it matters."

"I've had one bout of pneumonia, but other than that, I'm okay."

"That's the spirit. How's your grandmother?"

"She's fine. She'll outlive me."

"Don't say that. She's a very big woman. She's liable to drop dead of a massive heart attack any day now."

"Anyway, happy birthday," he said and gave me a chaste hug. He then turned in an extremely dignified manner and walked into the crowd where he soon disappeared. I watched him go and thought, Why would he do this to me on my birthday? Well, he was always selfish. Just like the time he didn't want to wear a condom. That old woman saved my life. I began to go over every other act of sex we ever had, dissecting it to see if there could have been any transmission. Soon, I was lost in paranoia as I struggled to remember if I'd had a cut on my finger that weekend. Just before I crashed into the bottom of the pit, something happened that stopped me. First of all, the No Tomorrow hit me like a huge wave of coloured water and then out of the surf, like Venus in the foam, stepped the boy from the Parthenon. He was smiling ear to ear and bopping around from foot to foot like a light-weight boxer. He was such a kid.

"Hey, dude. I heard it was your birthday. How old are you?"

For some reason, I answered truthfully. "Eight."

"Eight?"

"I was born in a leap year. I'm thirty-two."

"Wow, you don't look that old," he said.

"How old are you?"

"Nineteen."

"Wow, you look twenty," I said.

"Is that too young for you, dude?"

"It wasn't when I was thirteen. It might be now."

"Why? I had a great time the other night. I think you did, too."

"Oh, I did, believe me. It was wonderful."

"Then what's the problem?"

"I just don't have the time to educate a lover on top of giving him great sex. I tried it once before, and it didn't work out."

"I want you to teach me everything you know," he said with a straight face.

"Look, kid, you just got out of high school. Believe me, I'm a lot more complicated than geometry."

"I was great at geometry," he said and kissed me. All my reservations fell away. But I had a speech to make. Otherwise, I'd have to pay for my drinks. I told him to wait for me, and rushed onto the stage. This birthday was turning out better than I expected. I addressed the crowd.

"Welcome to my birthday. Tonight, we're just going to talk about how wonderful I am, and give me gifts. Something for everyone, but mostly for me. And that's the way it should be. The reason I seem so unnaturally greedy is because I was born on February 29, in a leap year, which means I only get a birthday every four years. Us leap-year children, or 'leapies' as we call ourselves in private, have been ripped off. We're just like the kids whose birthdays are on Christmas. We're filled with anger, which rules our lives, building up within us like a cancer, as we watch those around us collecting gifts year after year. For some leapies, this destroys them. Others find strength in it. I . . . am one of those." There was absolute stillness in the house. Except for about seventy fags in the back of the room still talking. Fags would be the only people in a hostage crisis not paying attention. Over the din, I heard one lone voice. It was Joey.

"It sounds like the No Tomorrow just kicked in."

"You got it, Lover Boy! Now where's my gifts?" The first person who came out onstage was Jack Maytag. He was an ultraliberal municipal politician in his early forties whose riding encompassed the gay community. He was straight, but good-looking enough not to have to be.

"This is for you, Buddy," he said, handing over a pizza box. "I may be mayor of this city one day, but you are already mayor of Gaytown." There was a smattering of applause. I opened it. Inside was a big pink triangle cookie.

"Oh, it's a freedom cookie. Thanks, Jack."

"I won't ask the lady how old she is."

"I'm no longer just a lady, Jack. I'm now a lady of a certain age."

"And what age is that?"

"Uncertain," I said. "You're so gorgeous, Jack." I turned to the audience. "Don't you wish he was gay?"

"I fucked him," came Joey's voice from the crowd.

"And you still didn't vote for me," joked Jack, playing the room like the seasoned politico he was.

"Okay, who's next?" I hollered, pushing Jack offstage before he stole the show. It was Donal, holding a paper bag. He handed it to me. I reached inside and pulled out a dildo.

"That's so thoughtful. How did you know my size?" I asked him, quickly moving on to the next presenter. It was Skeet Charles, a local gay playwright and agent provocateur. I had auditioned for him once, for the lead role in his musical production *Burr!*, the true story of Raymond Burr. I was perfect for the role, but I am convinced I didn't get the part because I wouldn't sleep with him. I had grown conciliatory toward him over the years, however, as I watched his career go into the toilet. He handed me a package wrapped in black leather. I unzipped it and pulled out another dildo, this one even bigger than the one before. It seemed like dildos were becoming the gay equivalent to socks at Christmas.

"Thanks for the socks, Skeet." He looked confused as I pushed him offstage.

"Okay, who's left?" Julius came out next. He was carrying a gigantic beautifully gift-wrapped box, which he could easily handle, as he was all arms. It looked like the kind of gifts actors give each other on soap operas. I was immediately suspicious.

"Buddy, on behalf of The Kennel, I would like to present you with a token of our appreciation. All you gotta do is pull this string," he said, pointing to a tiny string hidden in the ribbon.

"You're not going to fart, are you, Daddy?" He just grinned, and pointed to the string again. I pulled it, and all four sides of the box fell away, revealing a massive dildo the size of the caterpillar's toadstool in *Alice in Wonderland*. On it was written *The Kennel, 97 Isabella Street*. The man just couldn't stop advertising on cocks.

"I want the balls that go with it," I told him. All of a sudden, multicoloured smoke began to issue from the pisshole of the giant dildo. Soon the entire room was filled with smoke. The music started up, the lights began flashing, and everybody began to dance. I guessed twenty minutes had passed. Although by this point, I was so high I had lost all perception of time. I looked around for the boy but he was nowhere to be found. Then Julius insisted that I accompany him to his private office where "treats" were waiting. I went, vowing to look for the boy later. And finally, get his name. In Julius's office, Marco, Carma, and Joey were all waiting.

"Buddy, quick. Do three lines, catch up to the rest of us," urged Marco. I did and thoughts of the boy were pushed to the back of my mind. Everyone was gathered around listening to Joey. He was on a roll.

"I just got back from South Beach. Wow, what a scene. I had this one Cuban, Cesaro or something. He had this powder and we sniffed it. I thought it was coke, but it was Special K, and I went into a K-hole. It was like in a movie where the camera goes like this," he said, demonstrating by pulling his head back and then thrusting it forward. "I thought I was gonna die. It was great. Then we had sex, and I remember lying on his white leather couch with his big dick right down my throat. I'd just done a hit of poppers when the door opened and his roommate walked in. He was really hot, and he had a gram of coke on him. So we did that for a couple hours and we all had sex. But I didn't come. Then I went over to this guy's friend's house, and this friend had been up for two days on crystal. So I sucked his dick, but I still didn't come. Then I went back to the hotel but couldn't sleep. It was about eleven in the morning. So I went out by the pool and lay in the sun. Then I'm lying there with my eyes closed and I feel this grab and I open my eyes and it's the guy who had been up for two days. He says, 'You didn't come yet? Let's go upstairs.' What a nice guy! I fucked him without a condom. He wanted me to.

First, I didn't want to, but at this point, I figured it was his decision. I respect that."

At that moment, I realized Joey was positive. Life had gone from, "Is anybody gay?" to "Is everybody gay?" to "Is everybody positive?" I was glad I was wasted so I didn't have to deal with it. I was dimly aware of Marco and Carma Norma off in a corner, discussing the exciting new life-enhancing properties of blue-green algae.

"I have an idea," I proclaimed. "Party back at my place!" Soon, about thirty revellers were gathered outside the bar, raring to go. Even though I lived across the street, it took twenty minutes to get there, as the worst blizzard of the season had just hit town. In my stupour, I had completely forgotten about looking for the boy. When we finally got settled inside, the first thing we did was have hot cocoa and cocaine. White lines crisscrossed the surface of my black lacquer coffee table, creating a zebra pattern. Soon, everybody in the room was warm and toasted. Someone cleared a space on the floor and turned up the music. My possessions rimmed the dance floor like a levee. The boogying began. I got right into it, dirty dancing with every eligible male, which is everyone at a gay party. Then everybody insisted the birthday boy lead a conga line, so I obliged. We headed into the kitchen. There, we found a shirtless Julius chipping away at the ice that clung to the walls of the freezer. He looked angry. I had apparently forgotten to fill the trays. Marco was concerned because there were no more glasses, cups, or bowls to drink from, so I suggested shoes, as I had hundreds of pairs. We congaed on into my bedroom to get a few pairs and danced smack dab into Joey and George, Julius's lover, having sex. The conga line collided with the couple and reconfigured itself into an orgy. This would never have happened at Club Med. I would have joined in, but I was on a mission, so I grabbed what shoes I could, and went back into the kitchen.

"Here. Drink out of these," I said, handing Marco the footwear.

"Buddy, these are sandals. You've brought me dribble cups. Completely useless." I returned to my bedroom. The orgy had become locked in position, like a game of Twister.

"Buddy, can you help us?" said a little voice from the middle of the pile. I reached in and moved a hand off a buttock, and the entire mound fell apart.

"Thanks," said the same little voice.

"I was always good at Barrel of Monkeys," I said, gathering up more footwear. When I returned to the kitchen, Marco was sucking someone off.

"Here's your cups," I said.

"Buddy, as you can see I'm otherwise engaged. Go home."

"But it's my apartment."

"Go help Carma, then. She's fallen down between the couch pillows like a quarter." I wandered off in search of Carma and then went into a blackout. The next thing I knew, I was lying in my bed. I was completely naked and my Blue Boy costume was wadded up in a ball under my head. I turned and saw Joey fucking somebody next to me.

"Great party," he said.

"There wasn't enough ice," I replied.

"No one noticed."

"I did," said the guy being fucked. It was Julius. I could see that Joey wasn't wearing a condom. I got up and walked into the living room. There were a faggle of nude and seminude men, either passed out or groggily attempting to bring their flaccid dicks to orgasm. Feeling sick, I continued into the kitchen for a glass of water. This was going to be a bad hangover. I drank a gallon of water and then I had to pee, so I went into the bathroom. The sight that greeted me would have overwhelmed the Marquis de Sade himself. Lying facedown half-in and half-out of the tub was a naked man, his asshole being plunged furiously by the slender forearm of a kneeling figure with his back to me. I looked into the face of the man being fisted. I noticed that he was dead. He looked vaguely familiar except I'd never seen him dead before. Then the fister looked up at me and my heart skipped a beat!

It was the boy from the Parthenon. Well, I certainly had nothing to teach him. He smiled sweetly. I felt a cold wind pass through me as I suddenly remembered swallowing his cum.

"Hey, dude," he said. I had nothing to say. Yes, dear reader, I, Buddy Cole, was finally at a loss for words. Something inside me went crack and I felt my spirit begin to pull away from its frame with the distinct sound of Velcro separating. There was a brief sense of vertigo and then I left my body and floated up to the ceiling. I was having an O.B.E., an Out of Buddy Experience. People always said that I acted like I was above it all. Well, now I really was. I'd discovered the ultimate coping mechanism.

I floated back into the living room, looking for refuge from this symphony of horrors, but it was not to be. What greeted me there was the worst yet, dear reader. In the center of the room was a topless old woman with gold glitter eye shadow and white lipstick, spinning around and around on Rollerblades. The sight shocked me back into my body. I woke up days later in the hospital. Kate's face was staring down at me. She started in right away.

"Welcome back. You've been in a coma for four days. When they brought you in, your blood alcohol level was seven times past lethal. Your heart stopped three times. When they pumped your stomach, everybody in OR passed out. Later, they removed a gerbil from your ass. It was still alive, but don't even think about asking for it back. It is now in the custody of the humane society. A man was found in your tub, dead from a lethal combination of heroin, cocaine, ecstasy, and vanilla extract. He was forty-three years old, and worked as a teller at the Toronto Dominion Bank. He leaves behind a loving mother, three adoring sisters, and the Royal Monarchist League without an empress. But why would you care, Mr. Carefree? You don't care about anything, except yourself. From now on, either you shape up or ship out."

"Kate," I whispered hoarsely, "you're right. I have to go somewhere where people can accept me for what I am. Shallow! Can you get me a one-way ticket to Los Angeles, please?"

Granny
Limp
Dick

Once upon a time, there was a little girl who believed that the moon was made of green cheese, that hearts were made of butterscotch, and that someday her prince would come. One day, while sick at home with a cold, curled up in front of the television, a strange man burst in, drank all of her Neo-Citron, hogged the remote, shit on the carpet, and wiped his ass with her flannel nighty. After that, she didn't believe in fairy tales anymore.

Why am I telling you this, dear reader? Because I am that little girl. Life wiped its ass on my flannel nighty. But I took off that shitty garment and burned it, and all my illusions along with it.

I must confess, I had grown tired of gay life. All of its pettiness, shallowness, and emptiness weren't enough anymore. I needed less.

When I was a boy—well, I'm still a boy, but you know what I mean—I used to go to L'Isle des Memoires to remember things—birthdays, multiplication tables, where I last left Cornygirl. Now I was going to Los Angeles to forget—birthdays, multiplication tables, and whether or not I had AIDS. Plus, there was all that sun.

Meeting cute

In the artificial heart of Los Angeles beats a shopping mecca known the world over. It's called the Beverly Center. You've seen it in countless television shows and movies, from *Clueless* to that Bette Midler–Woody Allen multiple star pileup on the entertainment freeway, whose name escapes me at the moment. Actually, I do know the name of that movie, but it's bad luck to say it out loud. It's sort of like how stage actors will only refer to *Macbeth* as "the Scottish play." Actors in Los Angeles will only refer to this film as "the Mall movie." It's a curse that continues to this day. They say that Don Simpson had been watching it on laser disc the night he died.

I had been staying at a seedy way station for hookers called the Change the Sheets Motel, on Sunset Boulevard. I had been letting my hair grow and it was now almost shoulder length. Every day I would get up and walk to the Center, which is a couple of miles away. I would always be the only person on the street except for the homeless, hookers, and crazy people, but I had never learned how to drive so I had no choice. Despite the walking I was starting to pack on the pounds, but I didn't care as I had taken myself off the market. Once at the mall, I would head straight for the food court on the top level, where I would get myself a cappuccino and sit there, smoking and watching the world go by. Sometimes I would pay to see a movie, then hop from one multiplex screen to another, seeing as many movies as I could for the price of one. I was immersing myself in the world of movies of the nineties. What an education.

One day, after seeing a particularly good Hollywood movie about people and explosions, I was going down the escalator, lost in thought. Over six hundred people had died in the movie from different sorts of weapons, and I started to think about how marvelous it was that with the wonders of today's special effects you could show people dying so realistically. I thought about how impoverished I was as a child, not being able to see their guts and insides, like now. My feeling is, why bother with laborious dialogue that step by painful step slowly reveals a character's inner life, when you can just cut them open with a jigsaw and look inside for yourself? And what characters! Their guns had more personality. All the male stars of these action movies ever did was stand in front of a blue screen spouting one-liners. I could do that. I decided to become an action hero. Stardom was a given. I hoped the wrenching life experiences I had just undergone hadn't deepened my emotional range too much though.

All this was going through my mind as I rode down the escalator, so much so that I was waving my arms around in an attempt to collect my thoughts and bring them in for a safe landing, when my ring suddenly became ensnared in the titian tresses of a Beverly Hills Botticelli beauty going the opposite direction. She was wearing a yellow unconstructed Kenzo coat and her thick russet hair spilled over her shoulders and down her back like in a hair commercial, except in this commercial she was about to be scalped.

"Ow!" she yelled, grabbing her hair. Her head was yanked downward and my arm was pulled in the opposite direction. Our eyes met. It was my finger or her hair. The decision was

206 ❖ BUDDY BABYLON

made. She snapped her head back in a Highland Games kind of move and pulled me right off my feet and over the guardrail onto her side of the escalator, where I landed on my back on the razor-sharp edges of the moving stairs. We struggled our way to the top, a very polite and apologetic little Canadian and a big-haired woman cursing like a sailor. Suddenly my hand came free, complete with a lock of her hair. I sheepishly handed it back to her.

"I'm so sorry. This is yours." She tore it roughly out of my hand and tried to place it back onto her scalp.

"What the hell were you waving your arms around for?" she barked.

"I'm sorry. I was just trying to steady myself."

"Steady yourself? If you want to steady yourself, have a drink, don't fucking do the arm watusi on a busy escalator! You almost killed me. As it is, I'm going to probably have to have plastic surgery. Are you rich?"

"No."

"Fuck! Why can't the rich ever injure me? I'm an actress, you know. My hair is my living." I took a good look at her. She was in her mid-thirties, with flawless white skin, big brown eyes, a prominent nose, and lush, pouty lips. She had more than a few miles on her but still, a real babe. I suddenly placed her face.

"You're that actress I've seen in a million thankless parts. Tandy Porter. I'm always telling my friends, Why isn't she a star?"

"I am a star. What do you mean?"

"What I meant to say is, why aren't you a bigger star?"

"Yeah, well, that's the million-dollar question, isn't it?"

"You know what? I have a feeling that's all about to change."

"What do you mean?"

"Let me just say that there's a lot of buzz about you in town." I was totally bluffing, but I knew enough about actresses, being one myself, that she probably wouldn't be able to resist such a juicy worm.

"Everyone's saying, 'When is Tandy Porter going to explode?' And I say it will happen when she gets the right vehicle."

"That's what I'm always saying to my agent. Steiny, I say, get me the right vehicle, and I'll make you rich."

"I see you in a sitcom."

"A sitcom? I wouldn't lower myself. I'm a movie actress."

"Oh, so you're content to always be the seventh name in any given credit roll. Look. I'm a huge television star in my native Canada. You don't know me, but let me tell you, up there I'm as big as Sylvester Stallone so I know what I'm talking about. I was in a show called *Lookin' Around*. Every week, my character would look around. Very Canadian. It lasted for eight years, but this isn't about me."

"You're right. It's about me. Tell me more." An hour later, we were at the bar at the Mondrian Hotel, knocking back our third martini.

"You, in a sitcom, prime time, naturally, big ratings, giant press, spin-offs, huge hair," I sputtered excitedly. "So, your character I see surrounded by a lot of old guys. I don't know why. I just do. I'd cast a lot of Hollywood veterans who will work for scale again—Burgess Meredith, Red Buttons or Red Skelton, or maybe both. We need someone black. Ossie Davis. Maybe Dom DeLuise, get something queeny happening. That guarantees a guest spot for Burt Reynolds. Who knows? Take his toupee off and maybe he could be one of the regulars. Anyway, the point is, they are all hot to trot for you. You're like their teacher, teaching them how to paint. Or maybe a yoga instructor at a retirement colony in Miami, which means you could do a lot of Jewish schtick. That's always funny."

"Which one is the love interest?"

"Tandy, no. You keep them on a long leash. You don't have to fuck any of the old geezers. That would take away the

comedy. No, there's a sexy young doctor or hospital administrator. I got it! You play a sexy nurse in an old folk's home, and
your love interest is the place's administrator, played by someone like Ted McGinley."

"That's a lot of high-powered talent. Aren't you afraid they
might overwhelm me?"

"No, you have top billing. That's all that matters. Every
lion will shrink from the crack of the whip made by the sound
of your name above the title—Tandy Porter in . . ." I
thought for a minute. "Tandy Porter in *Chasin' Raisins.*"

"I love it," she exclaimed. "Especially that name above the
title thing. You're on the wrong side of the camera, you know.
You should be running a studio."

"I've been told that before."

"I wish you worked for me."

"Then I do."

Best first date in a comedy series

Morning, sexy," said a sultry, smoky female voice on the other end of the line.

"Is this Lauren Bacall?" I asked. "I told you I'm not interested in changing my long-distance carrier." Tandy laughed long and huskily. I pressed the receiver tight against my ear to feel the vibrations from her laugh deep inside my ear canal, causing an almost orgasmic eustachian pleasure. It was the closest thing I'd had to sex in months.

"Listen, you genius, you, my agent, Steiny, loved your idea and I've got a meeting next week with NBC."

"Congratulations. You deserve it. And you're going to get it."

"But that's not why I'm calling. I just want to know if you're free tonight."

"Always free for you, dear," I said, instantly intimate, Hollywood-style.

"Because tonight is the Emmy Awards. And my date fell through. So, I was wondering if you would like to accompany this rising young actress to the stinking thing because otherwise I wouldn't go. With you as my date, I figure it might be fun."

"I just happen to be wearing my tuxedo at this very moment. I fell asleep practicing Oscar speeches."

"Pick you up at four." This was unbelievable. I'd only been in Los Angeles a few weeks, and already I was squiring a star to an award show. What next? A very public overdose on a very busy street? Only the gods knew.

At four o'clock, Tandy's limo pulled up to the parking lot of the motel. I took her in with a glance. She wore a formfitting pearl-coloured Versace gown cut low in the back and slit up the sides. Her generous silicone breasts struggled to contain themselves within the scanty confines of the fabric, and her hair was piled up on her head in great whooshes of red and brown, grazing the ceiling of the limo. I was in goddess rapture.

"You look beautiful. You look breathtaking. My breath has been taken away. I literally have no breath. Please be less beautiful. Let me breathe."

"How's this?" She pushed back her nose and grunted like a pig.

"That doesn't help at all. I'm from a pig farm. Now you're just a beautiful pig. It's no good. I'm just going to have to learn to breathe without oxygen when I'm around you."

"Why are you staying at the Change the Sheets Motel?" asked Tandy, her nose wrinkling with disgust. "Only hookers and Charlie Sheen stay there."

"It's all I can afford."

"I thought you said you were a big star in Canada."

"I am, but you still only make about as much money as a security guard."

"I worked in Canada, once. I was in a David Cronenberg movie in the early eighties. All I remember about the role was a bug crawling out of my pussy. Definitely a low point for me."

"But a high point for Canadians." We drove for about an hour, drinking champagne and gossiping about the stars she knew. I noticed we were caught in a traffic jam of limousines, so I figured we must be close.

"Driver, are we almost there?" I asked.

"About five more minutes, sir," said the limo driver, who seemed kind of cute.

"Where you from?" I said, flirting a little.

"Toronto," he replied.

"Oh, you're both Canadian," said Tandy. "Driver. You must recognize my friend. He's a big star in Canada. Did you ever watch a show called *Lookin' Around*?" He glanced at me through the rearview mirror.

"No, never heard of it." I had to put a stop to this right away.

"Thank you!" I said abruptly, raising the glass partition. "Obviously one of those snobs who doesn't watch TV." Luckily, there was a commotion outside and the topic was quickly dropped. I lowered the smoked-glass window and looked out to see eight or nine ragtag Christians carrying hand-painted, misspelled signs saying such things as SODIMITES GO TO HELL! and AIDS IS GOD'S SALUTION TO HOMOSEXUALITY.

"Keep up the good work!" I yelled out the window. "Don't encourage them," said Tandy, pulling me back in. "How's my makeup? Do I look hysterically gorgeous or just ludicrously beautiful?"

"You look ridiculously stunning," I said. The limo pulled to the curb and the door opened. A man's arm reached in to help me out. I swung my tux-clad legs over the doorjamb and lowered my toes gently onto the first red carpet of my life. A gallant gentleman yanked me out of the car and the next thing I knew I was lying at John Tesh's size-fifteen feet. I picked myself up and turned around to see Tandy exiting the limo like a star. Lightbulbs popped and people behind huge barricades across the street yelled out her name. She waved, blew them a kiss, and came over to me. John thrust his microphone in her face.

"Tandy," he said. "What brings you to the Emmys? Haven't you always said you wouldn't do television?"

"What I said, John, is that I didn't feel that television had anything to offer me at the moment. Who knows? Maybe that moment has come."

"Are you saying you have a television project in the works?"

"We'll see," she said coyly.

"Come on, Tandy, give me something."

"Okay. I'm going to be married!" she announced.

"What?"

"Yes. I'd like you to meet my fiancé, Buddy Cole. He's a huge star in his native Canada." What was this? I thought.

"So is this official?" asked Tesh.

"Yes, John, I'm giving *ET* the scoop. I, Tandy Porter, after a lifetime of looking, have finally found the man of my dreams!" Suddenly, every reporter crowded around us, thrusting microphones and cameras in our faces. I turned to Tandy, dumbstruck.

"Just play along, Buddy. It's no big deal. Smile!" Caught up in the delirium of the moment, I grabbed Tandy and kissed her full on the mouth. A hundred cameras captured the image and a Hollywood couple was born. I had come to Los Angeles to become a star, but now I had found something even better. I could be the husband of a star. All the benefits of fame and none of the grief.

Tandy wasn't nominated for any award. She was just there doing regular career maintenance—seeing and being seen. We were seated in a midlevel celebrity section, about two thirds from the front of the stage. The ceremony was over three hours long and excruciatingly boring. The closest I got to being on camera was when I shoved my foot into Markie Post's close-up. The only really interesting part of the evening came when Tandy excused herself to go to the washroom during the Best Actress in a Situation Comedy category. She couldn't stand to watch any actress win any prize. As soon as she left her seat, some young guy plopped down beside me.

"Excuse me," I said. "My date is sitting there." It thrilled me to use the word "date." I wondered what base I would get to tonight. Was I already on first? I realized I knew so little about heterosexuality.

"Don't worry," he told me. "I'm a seat filler. My job is to make sure there are no empty seats in case the camera takes a shot of the audience. Nothing looks worse than gaps."

"Unless you're Lauren Hutton," I said. "What does that pay?"

"It's volunteer. We're just hoping to get spotted by some big producer."

"Isn't that nice." I couldn't believe my civility. Being straight was having a calming influence on me.

"I noticed you're here with Tandy Porter. That's really . . . interesting," he said, in an insinuating manner.

"How so?"

"Everybody knows. Tandy Porter is Hollywood's biggest—" At that moment, Tandy returned.

"Get lost," she said to the seat filler. He fled and she took her seat again. She was steaming.

"Fucking Jessica Tandy was in the cubicle next to me. She almost cleared the place. Old people's shit smells so bad. I don't care how gracefully you age, bowel movements always tell the tale."

After the awards there was a formal dinner. We sat at a table with Casey Kasem and his talented actress wife, Jean; ex-*Taxi* casting director Joel Thurm and his "friend," a handsome New York stage actor; former NBC honcho Fred Silverman, a silver fox going stag; Aaron and Candy Spelling, obviously still very much in love; and *Married with Children* costar Amanda Bearse with a beautiful Oriental woman named Jodi Chan. I couldn't eat any of my food as I was too excited by all the celebrities. So I just wandered around gawking. I got whiplash from constantly lookin' around. My technique was simple. I would sidle on up to a celebrity's table and stare at them from very close up, until security came to take me away. Then I would do it again. The system worked really well, until soon all of the celebrities were afraid of me. Before the end of the evening I was surrounded by fans and signing autographs as "Yours, the Stalker."

When I returned to the table, Amanda Bearse was nowhere to be seen. Tandy and Jodi were talking very close. I took the opportunity to look at Jodi. She was extremely beautiful and very pale, with a black pageboy haircut. She wore a robin's-egg blue silk gown that flared at the waist into an explosion of vermilion taffeta. She had kicked her high heels off and her bare toes delicately grazed Tandy's calf. There was a cute little tattoo of Casper the Friendly Ghost on her ankle. Tandy's nose was practically in her ear. What was this all about? I wondered. I toyed with my dessert. Tandy was completely ignoring me, so I made idle chitchat with Fred Silverman, who seemed lonely.

"Dessert's nice," I said.

"Yes. Very continental," he responded.

"I think it's got some rum in it."

"I think it's amaretto," he said.

"That's what it is. Amaretto. What's this crunchy thing?" Fred chewed a bit and considered it thoughtfully.

"Hazelnuts."

"You're right. That explains the amaretto connection. We've come full circle." We fell into silence. Then, Fred, because all television executives abhor a vacuum unless it's got at least a fifty share, tried to resume the conversation.

"Coffee's nice."

"Don't start up again, Fred," I said. Tandy and Jodi finally came up for air.

"Buddy, a bunch of us are going up to my place for a little get-together, and I want to know if you'd like to come."

"Well, we *are* engaged," I reminded her. We went outside, where a crowd was still gathered behind barricades. As we waited for our limo, fans yelled out her name. She clutched me closely, in a vague approximation of heterosexual bliss. I was in virtual heaven.

The morning after

After the awards Tandy, Jodi, and I piled into the limousine and drove back to Tandy's house in the Hollywood Hills—a sprawling three-bedroom bungalow just off Laurel Canyon. The place was exquisitely appointed with cool Moroccan tile floors, white walls, mirrors, and fresh-cut flowers everywhere. There were already a few people there, about four or five women who seemed to know the place really well. I was the only man there, which was fine. All those ladies to myself. We drank champagne and nibbled on ridiculously juicy fruit platters. There were no drugs, and no one drank too much except for me. But as I said, there were no drugs so I didn't beat myself up over it. We sat around and dished the awards. No one liked Julia Louis-Dreyfus's outfit, and we all felt that Oscar de la Renta was now low renta.

Tandy was definitely a different person away from the public eye. She didn't seem as hot for me as she was at the awards. She didn't even mention our being engaged to her friends. When I realized it was time to leave I asked Tandy to call me a cab, but she insisted I stay in the guest room. I was in no condition to argue so she took me upstairs, undressed me, tucked me in, and gave me a kiss good night. Second base! At this point, dear reader, you must be wondering: Has Buddy

Cole lost his bloomers? Isn't he the biggest fruit in the produce department? Does he really love a woman? Well, at the time I had to admit that I was down on men. Besides, Tandy had more balls than most men I'd been with. So I thought, what the hell. If I can't star in a Hollywood movie I'll star in a Hollywood marriage.

The next morning I woke up in a big canopy bed, facing open French doors revealing Los Angeles spread out before me underneath a thick sienna haze. Gorgeous. The door opened and I jumped. A well-built Mexican man in his thirties, nut brown and sporting a thick black mustache, entered the room carrying my two humble suitcases. He told me his name was Jesus, and that he worked for Miss Porter, who had ordered him to collect my things and pay my hotel bill. Things were working out even better than I'd dreamed. I went off in search of my intended. I heard murmuring at the end of the hall and walked toward it. The door was ajar and I peeked in. Tandy was propped up in bed, bare breasted, and drinking a carrot juice.

"Buddy, come in. Have you seen the *Hollywood Reporter*?" She held up a copy of the magazine. There was a full-page photo of us kissing at the Emmys. The caption said: Tandy Porter and Buddy Cole Engaged!

"Everyone's so happy for me. Now that I'm finally getting married," she said. Then a head popped up from under the covers. It was Jodi Chan. Oh, so that's what that was all about.

"You're getting married?" asked Jodi. "Great! I'm fucking a married woman!" The rest of the day was very hectic. First, I signed a prenuptial agreement, then we went to City Hall and got married before the justice of the peace. Tandy presented me with a huge wedding ring. I finally had that diamond. I couldn't have been happier. When we left City Hall the press was gathered on the steps outside. Oh, I'm sorry. I *could* be happier! We would only speak to John Tesh, though, in recognition of our long-standing relationship with him.

"Buddy and I have been friends since high school," she told him. "But we never even considered the idea of romance, until his wife sadly died of cancer last year and it brought us closer together. One day, we just looked into each other's eyes and knew that this friendship had blossomed into love."

"Are you going to take your husband's name, Tandy?"

"No. Even though I love him very much I will remain Tandy Porter. That's how my fans know me. And I love my fans!" People cheered.

"Mr. Cole, how do you feel about this?" asked John.

"Well, I'm old-fashioned, so I will be taking my wife's name. From now on, please refer to me as Buddy Cole-Porter." John Tesh let out a huge laugh, and I knew I was IN. The rest of the interview was a breeze, and when it was over he slipped us a cassette of his music. I kept it just in case I might ever need to torture a Viet Cong for information. Later that night, Jodi, Tandy, and I watched the segment on television from the comfort of Tandy's bitch-sized bed.

"You guys look like you're really happy," laughed Jodi. "You're a really good actor."

"I'm not acting," I told her. "I really am happy." And I really was. I was in a great marriage. Tandy was never home. She was always at the studio, her agent's, a yoga class, or some secret lesbian party. I was left alone at home in her fabulous house so I had to find ways to keep myself busy. I often found myself in the kitchen, not because I liked to cook but because there was a huge window over the sink which gave me the perfect vantage point from which to watch Jesus working shirtless in the yard. For weeks, the only thing the garbage disposal chewed up was my spunk. Then one day Jesus caught me masturbating to him and I realized that I needed an excuse to stay in the kitchen. So I got busy.

I started out creating exotic fruit juices in her space-age juicer, mixing them together into wild combinations. Then I started experimenting with mixing fruit, juice, and ice in the blender, and soon became quite adept at whipping together delicious and filling yet calorie-conscious fat-free drinks. One day, the muse told me to throw some milk and low-fat frozen yogurt into the mix and hit the puree button. What resulted was a brand-new form of beverage. I called it the smoothie, because it was smooth, and so was I. The first day I made my bride an orange–banana smoothie, she scoffed.

"I can't drink this crap first thing in the morning. It gives me the shits."

"That's the idea. Just try it. I added something special to it today. Some bee pollen, royal jelly, and an ounce of wheat-grass juice."

"Fine. I know you're trying to kill me. I'll just drink it and die already." She grabbed the glass out of my hand and downed it.

"Mmmm, not bad. I'm off. Kiss." She always said the word but never actually kissed me. A few hours later she called me from the studio office where she had recently signed a development deal. Her voice sounded like a young girl's.

"Buddy, that smoothie really works. I had the best bowel movement ever."

"Oh, I'm so happy to hear that. I can't wait for you to come home and tell me all about it."

"Can you fix another one? I'll send a driver. Actually, maybe you could make a few more. Steiny's feeling a bit loggy."

"It would be a pleasure, my princess. I'll put a little ginseng in it for extra zip. Will I see you tonight?"

"Maybe on the weekend. Love you. Love your smoothies."

"Love you," I said back, but she had already hung up.

*J*ather knows best

Tandy sat close beside me on the couch as I held her hand like a good husband. Both of us listened carefully to the words of the man in the black suit sitting across from us.

"Last month, a man named Beau Crosby fell off the roof of his mobile home in Fayetteville, Louisiana." Tandy gasped and squeezed my hand so tightly her nails drew blood.

"Upon investigation of the contents of his belongings, a document was found in which you were named as the mother of his twelve-year-old daughter, Miss Porter." Tandy fell back against the couch in an actressy swoon. I leaped to her defense.

"My wife doesn't have to sit here and listen to these wild accusations!"

"Buddy, it's all true," said an ashen Tandy. "I did have a child with that man."

"How could you!" I cried.

"I've sort of filed it away under 'forgotten' but I guess your past can't be escaped. I did a movie about that once, so you'd think I would know better. I gave her up because at the time I felt that he would be a better parent than me."

"He was an alcoholic biker who made crystal meth," said the lawyer.

"My point exactly. I was a long way from all this, let me tell you." She waved her hand at her home and furnishings, including me. "I had no job at the time. I was drinking more. I was a complete mess. Anyway, what do you want from me? As you can see, I'm recently married with a wonderful new husband, on the verge of starting a family of our own, and I just don't know if I can handle this. Financially or otherwise."

"Didn't I just read that you're about to star in a sitcom called *Chasin' Raisins* on CBS?" asked the lawyer. This was the first I had heard of it. It was my turn to draw blood.

"Is this true, darling?"

"Yes, Buddy, I forgot to tell you. I've been so busy getting ready for it, I guess it slipped my mind."

"I understand."

"Would you like to meet your daughter, Miss Porter?"

"Of course," she stammered insincerely. "Bring her in, we'll have one of my husband's famous smoothies, and then you can bring her back to wherever she now lives."

"I think she'll be living here, Miss Porter." Before we could react, the door opened and in walked our new daughter. She had long, flaxen chestnut hair tied back in a ponytail, and the open features of a sunflower. Her cheeks bloomed with health and her brown eyes sparkled like her mother's. She was about four feet tall and had a forceful personality. Well, one of her heads did. Yes, dear reader, Tandy's love child had two heads. Other than that, she was a perfectly normal little child. Or children.

"Which one of you cows is my mother?" screamed the head on the right.

"Miss Porter, I'd like you to meet your daughters, Suzanne and Pleshette," said the lawyer.

"Oh my God!" howled Tandy. "Oh, God! I never looked when they were born and Beau never told me. I was gone the next morning. Fuck, what a mess!" As head of the family I knew I had to take action before things got any worse. I went over to the girls and calmly introduced myself.

"Hello, Suzanne. Hello, Pleshette. My name is Buddy and I'm your new stepdad."

"Mom, are you married to a fag?" asked Suzanne, the one on the right.

"Shut up," said Pleshette to her other head. "You say that about everybody." She turned to me. "Hi, Buddy. Don't listen to her. She's just cranky because she's on the right side but she's left-handed." The left hand smacked Pleshette's head.

"Ow."

"Girls, don't fight. Your mother's had a rough day. She just discovered that she has a two-headed child that she abandoned twelve years ago. Besides being a hugh shock, this is going to play havoc with her official age. Let her rest." I turned to Tandy who was muttering to herself on the couch.

"Honey, I'm going to show the girls to their room." I turned to the man. "Thank you for all you've done. You can go. The girls are in good hands now." He hesitated.

"Miss Porter doesn't seem too pleased," he said.

"That's just the way she is. She doesn't use emotions in real life because she's an actress and doesn't like to bring her work home with her," I told him as I showed him to the door.

Over the course of the next few months Tandy was never home, as she was always working on her upcoming series, so I took the opportunity to play Daddy. Pleshette was soon my favourite although I tried not to show it. Suzanne was harder to love. I think something happened to her when she was little. The girls and I kept in touch with Tandy by reading interviews in which she would say how much motherhood had changed her. The press ate up Tandy's new image as the sainted mother of a handicapped child. Her career was really starting to happen, and I couldn't have been happier. I know I keep saying that but I really meant it this time.

Something new

One sunny California day Tandy came home. I hadn't seen her in so long I barely recognized her. It was like there was something new.

"Darling, what have you done? Did you get highlights?" I asked.

"No, darling, nothing so drastic as that. I had a nose job. I lopped off that horrid bump you hated so much."

"I never hated it."

"I know, but that's what the story says," she said, handing me a copy of the *National Enquirer*. The headline read: Tandy Porter Gets Nose Job to Satisfy Anti-Semitic Husband.

"I thought that was the best way to handle it. What do you think?"

"I'm not anti-Semitic," I said.

"I know. Here's a copy of the layout for next week's issue," she said, handing me a second copy. The headline read: Buddy Cole-Porter: I Love Jews!

"You'll love the story," she said. "It sounds exactly like you. Anyway, what do you think?"

"Why didn't you ask my advice first?"

"Why? You're not my husband."

"Actually, I am."

"Fuck off! What's done is done." I noticed the girls were watching from the doorway.

"Don't swear in front of the girls," I chastised her. She saw them and screamed.

"Ahhh! I'm still not used to them." She caught her breath and addressed the girls. "Don't sneak up on me like that. Call ahead before you enter a room." And with that, she fled. The girls looked at me.

"Are we Jews?" asked Pleshette.

"Apparently so," I answered.

"I want a nose job," announced Suzanne.

"You're too young for a nose job," I said. "Wait till you're at least as old as Tori Spelling was."

"But, Dad, our life expectancy is only sixteen," pleaded Suzanne. What could I say? My heart melted and I relented. When the bandages came off a week later I stood back and admired the doctor's handiwork. Suzanne had whittled her nose down to the size of a baby's fingernail. She looked like an alien, but I could tell she really wanted my approval so I lied.

"It's beautiful. Just enough to breathe out of. Everything else is excess, anyway." Pleshette seemed jealous.

"I want a nose job, too," she howled. "Otherwise people won't know we're twins."

"Okay," I said, giving in. A week later, when the bandages came off, I admired the same doctor's handiwork. Her nose was just as tiny as Suzanne's but Pleshette had upped the ante by having collagen injected into her lips. They ballooned like a blowfish. I could tell she wanted my approval, too.

"More to kiss you with." I could see Suzanne flaring up with jealousy.

"I want a lip job," barked Suzanne.

"No. Enough is enough."

"You love Pleshette more," she accused. What could I say? It was true, I did. I had to prove to Suzanne that it wasn't, so I let her get the lip job, and soon they were a matching set once again.

Foxes

I was having the time of my life playing Daddy to my princesses. But one night my fatherly responsibilities were really put to the test. The girls asked to borrow the car, and even though they were just twelve I figured they only had four more years to live so why not let them have some fun. I handed them the keys, hoping I was doing the right thing. I spent the entire time fretting in the kitchen with Jesus. He just kept saying to me that they were an abomination and should be put to death, which I thought was a bit harsh. Finally, at two o'clock in the morning the doorbell rang. I opened the door to the sight of a muscle-bound LAPD officer standing with my double delinquent. They looked drunk.

"They're okay, Mr. Cole-Porter," he said. "But it could have been a lot worse."

"Come in, Officer, and I'll make you a smoothie," I said. I turned to the girls. "Not a word, young ladies." We all filed into the kitchen.

"Would you like wheat grass, lecithin, bee pollen, royal jelly, protein powder, or blue-green algae added to your shake?"

"Do you have any creatine?" he asked.

"You're in luck. I just got some in today from a muscle queen in WeHo," I said, getting busy. "So what happened?"

"It seems the girls totaled your car on Mulholland."

"A car is just a lot of metal and plastic. The girls are okay and that's what's important."

"They were both drunk at the time of the accident."

"This is terrible. They know they're only supposed to drink at home. What am I going to do with them, Officer?" I said with the world-weariness of a television mother. I handed him a smoothie.

"Well, normally, I'd throw them in juvie hall and you and your wife would be charged with child neglect and would probably lose custody. But, since I'm such a huge fan of Miss Porter, I wouldn't do anything to jeopardize the debut of *Chasin' Raisins*, which according to *Entertainment Weekly* is the most highly anticipated new show of the season.

"Thank you so much, Officer. I'll bet your mother's proud." He finished his drink and got up.

"I trust, Mr. Cole-Porter, that you'll handle the situation from here on in."

"Yes. Thank you. And I think you'll find you have a lot more energy at the gym." He left. I turned on them immediately.

"What the hell were you two thinking?" I demanded.

"We were just partying," snarled Suzanne. "Besides, Mom hates that Infiniti. We did her a favour. I noticed the girls hadn't removed their coat.

"Take your coat off and stay a while."

"We're fine," they said in unison, which they never did. My father's intuition went haywire.

"All right. What's up? Take your coat off." They just stood there, their arms hanging slack at their sides. I had had enough. I grabbed their coat and yanked it off. I could not believe what I saw. Jutting out of their bony little girl's chest were two giant breasts, as hard and as unnatural looking as an adult film star's.

"I hope those are grapefruits," I said.

"We're sorry. We were drunk," said Pleshette.

"Whatever happened to getting a tattoo?" I exclaimed. "Oh, well. You'll have to deal with your mother some morning."

"What do you mean? She knew. It was her surgeon," said Suzanne.

"I give up!" I said, exasperated. "Make your own smoothies and make sure to clean up after yourselves. I'm tired of being your maid."

The next morning, we had a little talk. "After a good night's sleep, I realized that I'm going to have to live with your new breasts. It's just lucky he did such a good job. As for puberty, we'll cross that bridge when we come to it. I realize that all of your antisocial behaviour is just an attempt to get attention from your mother, so I've decided to throw you a party and I've invited your mother. How about that?"

"She won't come," said a sullen Pleshette.

"I promise you, she will. Look, I've realized that I was trying to buy your love but I've since discovered that your love is very expensive, so from now on I'm going to spend twice as much."

"We want a pony," said Suzanne.

"Don't aim so low. I'd have asked for an elephant." I enlisted Jesus' help in transforming the backyard into a circus tent. In addition to the pony and elephant, I got a clown and two plate spinners from Taiwan. I even had it catered by Wolfgang Puck. There was everything from bubble gum–flavoured foie gras for children, to a cake shaped like a two-headed teddy bear. Eat your heart out, Cody Gifford. The girls even allowed me to redecorate their room. The first thing I did was tear down that Confederate flag they had hanging over the window. I was their father now. The second thing I did was remove all the empties. With the money I got back I papered the room with *Anne of Green Gables* wallpaper imported from Japan. I dare any child to do bad in front of Anne. At 2:00 P.M., the first guest arrived. It was a little girl, about ten years old, who looked about eighty. She was one of those kids who had the aging disease. I recognized her from the *National Enquirer*.

"Hi, what's your name?" I asked sweetly.

"Gaby," she croaked.

"Well, come in, Gaby." She barged by, stepping on my foot.

"Where's Plesh and Sue?"

"Just go on through to the backyard," I said, motioning toward the French doors. The doorbell rang again. This time, it was a teenage boy, with sandy-brown hair, bright-green eyes, and skin the texture of an alligator's.

"Hi, what's your name?" I asked.

"Alligator Boy."

"Not your stage name. Your Christian name."

"I told you. It's Alligator Boy."

"Did your parents call you that after seeing that you had alligator skin?"

"No, it was just a coincidence. Where's the babes?"

"Just go on through to the backyard," I said. The doorbell rang again. This time, it was a towering baby boy accompanied by a Latin nanny. It was "Carlos the Brazilian Super-Baby." I gushed.

"Carlos, I love you. I read your story in the *Globe* and I cried. How's your family? Does your father have a job yet? Have they finally gotten you a proper bed?" I was starting to well up.

"He's a baby. He can't talk," said the nanny in a thick Brazilian accent. "Where's the elephant? The Thing with Two Heads said there would be an elephant."

"It's in the back," I said, showing them the way. The party was a disaster. When the clown saw the children, he quit.

Then, the Taiwanese plate spinners claimed that Alligator Boy was a bad omen predicted in one of their folk tales. They quit, too, but not without demanding more money than we had agreed upon. I didn't have it, so I gave them some of Tandy's best plates. She wouldn't miss them.

The girls refused to ride the pony, saying it smelled. Carlos was the only one to take a ride, but his weight caused the poor pony to go into a spasm and a pet chiropractor had to be called. Gaby scared everyone. In fact, when Jesus saw her he crossed himself, went to his room, and stayed there for the rest of the day. On top of it all, no one touched the food. I discovered why when I walked into the washroom without knocking and found Gaby and Alligator Boy inside, doing a huge rail of coke.

"You can't have any. It's prescription," she yapped. After getting the doctor's name I threw them out. Tandy was a no-show, but she did send a telegram, which the girls tore up. At the end of the day, when all the guests had gone home and the last elephant turd had been picked up, I sat on the edge of the bed and tucked the girls in.

"Doesn't Mommy love us?" asked Pleshette.

"Yes, she does, very much."

"I hate her. I hope she dies and they bring her back to life and kill her again," cried out Suzanne.

"Don't say that about your mother. Think it. But don't say it. Now I want you two to go to sleep, and tomorrow we're going to your mother's plastic surgeon and see about getting those eyes done."

"Yay! More work," they said, snuggling in.

"Then later, Daddy's going to have something done, too. Why should I miss all the fun?"

"What are you going to get, Daddy? Liposuction?" asked Suzanne. I looked down at my spare tire, which had grown during my marriage.

"No, I'm going to have an HIV test."

"I want one, too," said Pleshette.

"No, it's for grown-ups."

"Kids get AIDS, too. It's not just a gay disease," she pleaded.

"Okay, you can both get tested. Now go to sleep." And as I closed the door I listened to them talking quietly in bed.

"If I have AIDS, you do, too," said Suzanne.

"No, I don't," cried Pleshette.

"Yes, you do. We have the same circulatory system."

My girls.

A modest business proposal

One day a few weeks later, Tandy's driver neglected to show up to get her smoothie order. So I decided to bring them down myself. Tandy's show was being shot at the CBS Radford lot in Studio City. When I told the security guard that I was Tandy Porter's husband I could barely contain my pride. As he waved me through, I felt like Mickey Hargitay visiting Jayne Mansfield on set. After a bit of searching I finally found Tandy's dressing room. I took a moment to look at the star with her name on it. Then I knocked.

"Come in," said my love sweetly. When I opened the door, her tone changed.

"What the fuck are you doing here?"

"Your driver never showed up, so I brought your smoothie myself."

She changed again. "Oh, honey, you are too wonderful."

What an actress! The very definition of "mercurial." The bathroom door opened and out walked a big-breasted blond girl.

"Buddy, I want you to meet Tawney."

"Would Tawney like a smoothie?" I asked.

"Yeah, sure," she said, tasting it. "This is delicious. Did you make this? What's in it?"

"Well, fresh-squeezed cactus pear juice, beet tops, parsley, pine gum, ma huang, ice cubes, skim milk, and cayenne pepper. I call it the Desert Pepper Rag."

"Wow, I can feel it in my breasts," she said. I was right. Cayenne pepper can penetrate silicone. At that moment, a wizened apple-doll face peeked through the crack in the door. It was Burgess Meredith.

"Hey, baby, hurry up. We're rehearsing our big scene."

"Burg, have you met my husband, Buddy?" said Tandy, returning to her makeup mirror.

"No, pleased to meet you. What's that you got there, kid?" he said, indicating the beverages.

"They're smoothies. Would you like one?"

"Sure." He gulped it down. "This is good. Got any more?"

"No, I'm all out, but I could bring more tomorrow."

"I'd like some more, too," said Tawney. "How much are they?"

"Oh, don't be ridiculous. I couldn't imagine charging money for them. It just gives me pleasure to see people drinking tasty, healthy things." Besides, I didn't need the money. Being Tandy's husband paid very well. The next morning I packed up the car with everything I needed and drove to the lot. The security guard recognized me.

"Here, have a Blueberry Jumper," I said, handing him a bright-blue tumbler.

"Thanks, Mr. Cole-Porter. You're the top!"

"Sometimes I'm the bottom!" I went in and set up a little smoothie stand next to the craft services table. I set out all my props and put up a little sign saying FREE SMOOTHIES. It was an instant hit. By midafternoon, the line spilled out of the studio and onto the set of *Roseanne*. When Roseanne saw her cast and crew enjoying the beverages, she decided she wanted one, too.

"I want a juice NOW!" she bellowed.

"It's actually not juice. It's a smoothie. Fresh juice is just one of the components," I replied calmly.

"Don't argue with me! You're fired!"

I answered her by thrusting a smoothie in her face and she took a sip. She actually smiled as one of her nicer personalities emerged.

"Wow. That's delicious. What's in it?"

"Fresh papaya, carrots, soy milk, wheat germ, ice, and special for you, some antipsychotic medication."

"Thanks. Maybe now I can get through this fucking day."

"Make sure you drink all of it. Medication settles," I called out to her as she walked off. Next in line stood a towering woman who looked familiar. I realized with a start it was my sister Pascal. With the exception of Pierre, I had not seen a family member since I left home all those years ago. She looked the same as always to me, only she was shorter now because she stooped more.

"Buddy. Son of a bitch, give me a hug." We embraced.

"What are you doing in Los Angeles?" I asked her.

"I'm a camera operator on *Roseanne.*"

"That's fantastic. I'm so happy for you."

"So you got married to Tandy Porter, eh? I must say I was surprised to read that in the *National Enquirer*. You didn't seem like the marrying kind growing up."

"Well, things change. Have you heard from anyone back home?"

"Oh, yes, Buddy, it's terrible, eh, what's happening. The farm has almost gone under."

"Oh, no. Why?"

"Nobody eats pork anymore. Everybody's gone healthy. Even up there."

I looked with guilt at the smoothie in my hand. "Who's running the farm now?"

"Guy," she said. "He doesn't know what he's doing and I can't help. He drinks, eh? I send what money I can, but it's not enough. It's hard, because I work on *Roseanne* so I'm always getting fired and rehired."

"Okay, break's over," said Roseanne, sweeping through and collecting her crew.

"I gotta go," said Pascal. "I'm really glad to see you. You need your family in this place, eh?"

"Yeah." She started to go and then turned back one more time.

"Hey, remember. It all started with you, eh. The prettiest feet. Thanks."

"Where's that giant French freak?" yelled Roseanne from somewhere within the soundstage.

"I got to go. *Au revoir.*" We hugged tightly and Pascal lumbered off to resume work. The next day when I arrived, the security guard told me that there was a small electric cart waiting for me. It turned out to be from Jason Alexander on *Seinfeld.* He wanted me to race over and meet him on the soundstage. He had heard about the smoothies and wanted something special. As I rode over, I conjured up a special recipe for him in my head, a special diet chocolate smoothie made from carob and licorice root with ginkgo biloba for mental alertness and yohimbe root for virility. I hoped he wouldn't take that the wrong way. He didn't. He loved his smoothie, especially after I told him he was the best thing on the show. Flattery. That's the real special ingredient.

Soon, every star on the lot was demanding designer smoothies, each one developed for their own very specific personality traits. I became so big that the production company Brillstein-Grey offered to set me up in business. But I said no. I didn't want this to become another "Newman's Own."

The *Chasin' Raisins* premiere date finally arrived. Some mysterious bigwig with a yacht offered to host the event. The guest list was very hush-hush and very exclusive. Only Hollywood's biggest movers and shakers were invited so absolute secrecy was a must. When we got out of our limousine down at the docks and I saw the ship, I couldn't believe it. It was the size of the royal yacht, the H.M.S. *Britannia*. I could barely suppress my excitement as Tandy and I made our way up the gangplank. A beautiful woman led us into a screening room. Already in attendance were John Travolta and Kelly Preston, Tom Cruise and Nicole Kidman, Kirstie Alley and Parker Stevenson, Juliette Lewis, Isaac Hayes, Lisa Marie Presley, Nancy Cartwright (also known as the voice of Bart Simpson), and countless other non-celebrities, more commonly known as "people." Everyone was very friendly. I couldn't believe it. It didn't seem like Hollywood at all.

Tandy went to the front of the room and made a little speech, and then the episode began. Tandy played the role of Nurse Tandy Lewis and she nailed it. She got every laugh in the script and then some. The old guys were by turns poignant, funny, and incontinent. Everything you want from a show-biz veteran. Richard Hatch, in the role of the hospital administrator, made you totally forget *Battlestar Galactica*. It was a complete success. When the show ended and the credits began to roll, I lay back against my seat filled with pride. I knew that we had done it together. And that's when I saw the final credit: FROM AN ORIGINAL IDEA BY L. RON HUBBARD. I exploded.

"Hey, wait a minute. *Chasin' Raisins* was MY idea."

"Calm down. We'll talk about this later," she said with a chill.

"No, we won't!"

"You're starting to make a scene," she said. Everyone pretended not to hear except Kirstie Alley, who was sitting behind us. She leaned over the back of the seat with concern etched into her mobile comic's face.

"Can I be of help?" she asked.

"Shelley Long was better!" I yelled at her. Tandy grabbed me by the arm and marched me into the bathroom.

"Who the hell do you think you are, behaving like this on MY NIGHT? I've given you everything. You have a home, a pool, children, a Mexican. You're living the California dream. And what do I get from you? A hissy fit! In front of all my friends. Look, I'm out there working my ass off every day with a bunch of fading fart machines to give you a nice life and what do you do? Run around like some granny limp dick in a golf cart making blender drinks for my rivals with ingredients paid for by ME! It's not fun anymore, is it, Buddy? It hasn't been fun in weeks. This marriage isn't working out. I want a divorce."

"Fine. I'll be gone in the morning. Oh, and Tandy? Congratulations on *Chasin' Raisins*. I hope one day, when you are a raisin, you'll look back on your days as a grape with regret." I thrust my chin in the air and walked out. When I got home there was a letter from Marco. I tore it open and read it.

> Dearest Buddy,
> It is with a heavy heart that I write this letter to you. Last Saturday past I went over as per usual to Carma Norma's for our weekly blowout. When she didn't come to the door, I was alarmed, so I used my key. The living room and kitchen were empty, so with great trepidation, I pushed open the bedroom door. I found Carma on her hands and knees on the floor, completely naked and completely dead. Upon closer investigation, I discovered that her face was buried in a pair of Carma Norma Bum Pads for Men, and upon even closer investigation, I discovered that they used to be mine. Clutched in her hand was a bottle of poppers and a Polaroid that you took of me showing my asshole to you on that trip we took to Fort Lauderdale. I always wondered where that went. Buddy, you were wrong. Someone did love my bony ass. Ah, Carma. She died as she lived—with dignity. The autopsy revealed that she died of a massive heart attack brought on by excessive amounts of cocaine and poppers. It's really been a wake-up call for me. I've vowed not to use poppers after a big night of doing blow anymore. The old ticker can't take it.

Anyway, it was a lovely funeral, and everyone says hi.
We're wondering if you ever plan on coming up for a visit.
We're going to have a memorial for Carma in a few months.
Something a little less formal. You know, no religion, and some
treats. Maybe you can make it. We read about your marriage
in the tabloids. Have you completely lost your bloomers? Tell
me it's not true, but seeing as how you never write, I guess I'll
never know.

I'm doing good. By the way, I finally got tested for AIDS,
and guess what? I'm negative. But I knew that already. How
about you?

Love and kisses, Marco.

The letter left me completely confused as to what to feel.
On the one hand, I was sad for the death of Carma, but on the
other hand I was happy that Marco had tested negative. Not
being able to choose, I decided to feel paranoid instead and
remembered my HIV test results languishing at the doctor's
these last few months. I had to know. I decided to bring a
special smoothie along for the doctor in case it was bad news
and he couldn't handle it.

"Mmmm, this is really good. What's in it?" he asked.

"Fresh beet juice, watercress, echinacea, ice, and low-fat
yogurt."

"Well, it's a real pick-me-up. Could I make this at home?"

"Sure."

"I can really feel the echinacea."

"Dr. Weil, I wonder if you have the results of my HIV
test."

"Oh, yes." He studied a piece of paper and smiled. "You're
negative, Mr. Cole. Boy, this is delicious."

"You know, Doctor, you can heal yourself just by eating
right. Eight weeks to optimum health, I always say."

"That's interesting. Well, good day, Mr. Cole." Years later,

Dr. Weil was on the cover of *Time* magazine selling my philosophy. I've really got to start copyrighting my brainstorms.

After testing negative, I decided to return home. My marriage was over, and my seed wasn't radioactive. I was free. First I would go to Toronto to see Marco and Kate, and attend the memorial, and then on to St. Hubert sur la Lac to save the farm.

The divorce was very quick. I pleaded no contest and I was out of that marriage in a week. As agreed upon, I got nothing. She even kept the diamond ring, giving me back my goal in life. Since I wasn't the natural father of the girls, custody was given to Tandy. I was sad to see them go, especially Pleshette. I hoped that she would come visit me during the holidays. As long as she came alone.

Revelations

Well, dear reader, if you're still here, then you're the best listener I've ever had. I think I'll keep you. I feel by now as if we know each other, even though I've done all the talking. One day we'll sit down and you'll tell me all about yourself—your hopes, your dreams, your bloopers. But that time is not now. No, cherished reader, we are at long last in the home stretch of *Buddy Babylon*. Soon all your holes will be filled.

When I came into this book, I was but a mewling babe in a pork pie. I grew into a sturdy effeminate lad. Countless adventures followed, and many lessons were learned, some of them very hot. More countless adventures followed. At times, you thought you were going to lose me, didn't you? But I hung in there. I had a story to tell, by golly. What I'm trying to say is that every step of this journey of mine has been taken not for myself, but for you. My God, I just realized something. I'm the only truly selfless person I know. What a revelation.

We have but one thing left to do—return home, where it all began, and tie up the loose ends. It's the least I can do. And you can return the favour by writing to Bantam Doubleday Dell, care of the evil editor, demanding that Buddy Cole receive a huge advance on the inevitable sequel. Thank you for being my friend.

The ballad of carma norma

Toronto had changed tremendously since I had been gone. It seemed like they had just been waiting for me to leave so they could put up some new buildings. I directed the cabdriver toward my final destination, Xingu's newest restaurant, Failures, on Queen Street. It was Toronto's first broth-only restaurant. I was really looking forward to his famous chicken-feather and cloves broth, which all my L.A. actor friends had raved about after tasting it at the last Toronto Film Festival. This was the location of the memorial for the late Carma Norma, which I had flown in to attend. My plane was late and traffic was heavy, so I urged the Sikh driver to speed up, but he wouldn't. I knew I was back in Toronto.

Finally we arrived. I gave the driver a tip, a simple mayonnaise treatment you could make at home for turban-damaged hair. I went inside. Like every one of Xingu's restaurants it was exactly of the moment, but since I didn't know what that moment was anymore it made no impression on me. The first thing I noticed was a giant photograph of Carma Norma at the far end of the room. It was a picture of her as a young woman holding the prototype pair of bum pads as though they were the stone tablets of the Ten Commandments. The photo was extremely unflattering, but I vowed to keep my mouth shut, because you should never speak ill of the dead unless you had actually killed them. There were people sitting on folding chairs facing the picture, and someone at the front was about to begin a speech. It was Marco. I quietly took a chair at the back and listened.

"Dearly departed. We are gathered here to celebrate the life of one Carma Norma. I met Carma on my very first modeling assignment. I was a young, naive lad from Ottawa who was determined to crack the modeling world, and she was a humble wardrobe assistant. We hit it off right away and became instant friends. My career stalled after a promising start and soon I was losing job after job and didn't know why.

"Then one day, some sniveling pantywaist of a photographer who shall remain nameless said, 'Mr. Nagy, you have no ass.' Though cut to the quick, I knew it was true. I told Carma about this, and for a woman with more than enough ass for the both of us she really seemed to understand. She had that ability to empathize with those less fortunate than her. And Carma, who lived to help others, set about to find a solution.

"Not two days later, Carma presented me with a box. Inside were two foam rubber pads, each shaped like a buttock. They fit like a charm, and when I looked at myself in a full-length mirror in a pair of jeans, I knew my dark days were over. Now there had been bum pads before, but they were crude and uncomfortable things and more importantly, they were always only one piece. Carma's particular genius was that she understood that, just like breasts, one cheek is always bigger than the other, so her solution was two adjustable bum pads.

"We all know the rest of the story. They took off, and she became a multimillionaire. But she never changed. She remained the same Carma Norma I had always known. Giving and selfless. She always said to me, 'Marco, I owe everything to you and your flat ass.' But the truth is, dear friends, it is I who owe everything to her and her fat ass."

By this time, he was weeping uncontrollably. There was

sniffling throughout the room, but not all of it was from sorrow. Marco started to move through the crowd, shaking hands and hugging people. At first he didn't see me so I took the opportunity to appraise him. Frankly, he had gained a few pounds. I made a mental note to myself not to mention it. Then he saw me and his face lit up.

"Buddy, you came," he sobbed, throwing his arms around me. "Carma's dead."

"I know, but gaining weight won't help. Oh. I'm sorry, I didn't mean to say that. People say strange things around death."

"I see nothing's changed. Still the shark. Now, more importantly, where's that Hollywood wife of yours? I love *Chasin' Raisins.*"

"We're divorced."

"Tragedy all 'round. God, it's good to see you. Come and say hi to some old friends." We went into the kitchen where Xingu was labouring away stirring a giant cauldron of broth. It smelled like the inside of a cast. My mouth began to water.

"Hey, Buddy, been a long time. Did you bring your wife?" asked Xingu.

"No, we're divorced."

"Shit, I really wanted to meet her. I love *Chasin' Raisins.*"

"I created it, you know."

"Ah, Buddy, there you go again, taking credit for everything. I suppose you invented the bum pads, too," said Marco. At that moment, in walked Laughter, Cunt, and their friend Zoriella. I hadn't seen them in years but they looked even younger. They had had more work done.

"Hi, Buddy. You look wonderful," said Cunt in a soft voice.

"You do, too, Cunt," I said.

"Oh, my name's Anne now. I changed it because the union wouldn't put my name on credit rolls."

"Why, because it's obscene?"

"No, because it's already taken. Laughter's still named Laughter, though," she said, laughing.

"Oh, Laughter, how I've missed you," I said, hugging her.

"I'm Zoriella," said the girl I was hugging.

"I'm just joking," I said, but I actually couldn't tell them apart. They had had so much plastic surgery that they had all turned into the same woman.

"Well, let's go, we've got a lot of catching up to do," Marco said to me. We drove over to Carma's mansion in Rosedale in her car, a black Porsche. She had left it to Marco in her will, along with everything else. Marco was now a very rich man. Carma's house was beautiful, and Marco had been staying there since her death, sorting out her affairs. He was executor of her will. Her family in Florence, Italy, hadn't had any contact with her for thirty years, but now that they knew she was wealthy they were suddenly bereaved.

"I suppose the millions help take away the grief, but I'd give back most of it to have Carma with us again. I miss her that much, I do," said Marco, opening the door. I walked into the house and looked around. Oddly enough, this was the very first time I'd been to her home. I was amazed to discover that she had exquisite taste. In the living room hung a huge Botero painting of an obese, naked woman. Maybe Carma had more self-awareness than I had ever given her credit for. I regretted not getting to know her better when she was alive. Maybe I could get to know her now that she was dead.

"Come, I'll show you around." The next room we went into would have made a librarian come. All four walls were lined with shelves, which groaned with books of all kinds.

"She always had her nose in a book," he said. "She read every one of these. One day, I tested her. Spent the whole afternoon pulling out books and asking her what they were about. We were so high. But she still knew every one."

"But you've never read a book. How would you know if she was right or wrong?"

"What?" It had never occurred to him that she might have been bluffing. Then he turned somber. "You never liked her."

"Yes, I did. I just didn't think we had a lot in common. She always seemed so. I don't know, stupid around me."

"That's because she was intimidated by you. She always thought you hated her." It's amazing. You know someone for almost fifteen years, and yet you don't know them at all. If you had asked me whether Carma Norma had ever read a book, I would have said maybe a cookbook. What I couldn't understand was how a woman who went around looking as bad as she did could somehow surround herself with such impeccable style at home. Marco asked me to stay with him, and since I didn't have any money I accepted the offer. That night, lying in bed, I gave Kate a call.

"Chuck, you fucker. I haven't heard from you in years. How's life with the movie star?"

"We got a divorce. Haven't you heard?"

"Not everybody reads the tabloids."

"You sure it wasn't mentioned in the *Utne Reader*?"

"Ha ha ha. How long you here for?"

"Not long. I hope to leave by week's end. I'm going home, Kate, to St. Hubert sur la Lac. They need me. How about you? Want to come with me? I'll bet you're unemployed."

"I'll bet you are, too," she replied. "Sure. I'd love to see the town that spawned the likes of you. Call me tomorrow and we'll make plans. Good night."

Northern barrymores

The roar of the twin-propeller bush plane made conversation impossible. Every now and then, Kate would bellow something in my ear, and I would just nod and smile, pretending to hear. We flew at an altitude of just three thousand feet, so the view was magnificent. But for most of the trip, I was transfixed by our pilot, Barclay Kent, Canada's only black bush pilot.

Even though the plane seemed to be made out of balsa wood and the door beside me was secured with duct tape, I felt safe. Even though Barclay was navigating with a crude map drawn on a bar napkin the night before, I felt safe. Even when the motor stopped for ten seconds, I still felt safe. Maybe it was because Barclay had the authority of General Patton and the face of a *Thunderbirds Are Go!* puppet.

He was from Halifax, a political science dropout from the University of Toronto. He'd had a summer job flying a bush plane and loved it so much he never went back to school. Now he flew geologists, doctors, natives, government workers, celebrities, and anyone else who asked all over the north. He was also recently divorced from his wife, a mildly amusing op-ed columnist for the *North Bay Nugget*. He loved Bruce Springsteen, Labrador retrievers, boxing, and the writings of Belva

Plain. How did I know all this? I had gleaned it all the night before in the Porcupine Lounge of our hotel in North Bay when the three of us had gotten roaring drunk.

I had to admit, watching him work the controls made me realize how much I had missed being with a man. I knew he was straight but still, there was this Belva Plain thing. I wondered if there was a chance. I felt my sap rising again. Maple syrup season was nigh.

Soon we came upon Lac d'Eau. It looked exactly as I remembered it. Thank God water doesn't change. Of course all the fish had probably died from acid rain, but it still looked pretty. We hit the water with a thud, and I clutched Barclay's thigh. He let it stay there as we skipped roughly across the lake like a stone. When we finally came to a halt he turned to us.

"I thought we were going to crash," he said matter-of-factly.

"You did? But you seemed so together," I said.

"Inside, I was shitting my pants."

I laughed. We taxied up to our old dock and got out. I looked toward the house. It seemed quiet. Kate and I grabbed our things and bid Barclay good-bye. He was off to spirit Kurt Russell and Goldie Hawn to their cottage on Lake Rousseau in the Muskokas. I told him to tell Kurt that I just loved *The Computer Wore Tennis Shoes.* He said he would be back in the district next week, so I told him to stop in. Then, getting back in his plane, he gave me the thumbs-up and I returned it. I felt like a jock.

"You're wasting your time. He's straight," said Kate.

"He let me touch his thigh in terror. Besides, I'm just being friendly. Can't a gay man be friendly to a straight man without everyone rolling their eyes?" She responded by rolling her eyes.

"That's the first time I ever saw you roll your eyes, Kate. It looks good on you. I always said lesbians should use more facial expressions."

"It's hard with you around, stealing them all."

"Don't hate me for being animated." The two of us walked up toward the house. The first thing we came across was the barn. It looked pretty much the same. It had always been in terrible shape. We went inside. My mind flooded with memories, but memories were all there were because the barn was empty except for one morose-looking pig in a pen. She looked up from her mud pack and I noticed that she had extraordinarily long eyelashes. She'd have been a real looker if she wasn't so glum. She blinked her eyes a few times and I could swear she was appraising my outfit. I think I passed because she pushed herself up and came over to lick my proffered hand. It felt sensual. I was so horny from the plane ride with Barclay, this pig was turning me on.

"Let's go before I do something I regret."

"Pretty pent up, eh? Me, too. Two years for me."

"Same here."

"What? You? Bullshit!"

"It's true. Tandy and I tried but she was frigid." Kate chortled and punched me a little too hard in the shoulder. I took it like a man.

We continued on to the house. As we got closer, I could see it was a shambles. The paint was chipping off. Windows were broken, and some were even boarded up. The grass hadn't been cut in ages and almost reached our waists. I went to the door leading into the kitchen, grabbed the rusty knob, and went in. There was Guy, sitting at the kitchen table, drinking. He looked better than he did when he was young. He had grown into his ears. He noticed me enter and as if no time at all had passed, started in on me.

"Well, well, well, look who it is. If it isn't Mr. Hollywood! Have you come back to laugh at us?"

"Nice to see you, too. What happened to all the pigs? There's just one left."

"You mean Persephone. She's all the livestock we have. I don't have the heart to kill her."

"Buddy!" said Fleur, coming into the room. We hugged. She looked like Maman, if Maman hadn't smoked or drank. "You've been gone so long, and you never wrote, and we never heard from you. What made you come home?"

"I saw Pascal in Los Angeles, and she told me what was going on," I said. Guy exploded.

"And what *is* going on, Mr. Hollywood? You tell me! Did she say I was a big drunk? Did she say that I'm going to lose the farm? Did she tell you nobody eats bacon anymore?" I remembered that Kate was hovering in the doorway. Guy pointed at her.

"Who's that?" he asked.

"That is my friend Kate. This is my brother Guy, and my sister Fleur." Kate nodded.

"Your problems are over. I've come back to help," I said dramatically.

"What are you going to do? Dance in the woods? Wear a funny hat?" said my brother.

"I've got money," I said.

"No, you don't. We read all about the prenup," said Guy.

"Buddy, what were you thinking?" asked Fleur incredulously. "Were you in love?"

"I was in like. You do crazy things. What about you, Fleur? Did you ever get married?"

"I just never got around to it," she said, blushing.

"Maybe you're not the marrying kind," said Kate. She hadn't been there two minutes and already she was hitting on my sister. Dykes! They're so slutty.

"How long are you planning to stay?" asked Guy.

"I don't know. I have to figure out what I'm going to do."

"Well, you better hurry, Mr. Hollywood. The bank is fore-closing on the mortgage at the end of the year."

"Well, that gives me plenty of time for my plans," I said.

"What plans?" asked Fleur hopefully.

"My plan to save the farm. I can't say any more." The truth was I didn't have any plans but I couldn't let them know that. They were depending upon me. Well, Fleur was. I couldn't let my family down again. I would do it for Maman and Papa. Whatever "it" was. I hoped that the familiar surroundings would trigger something. All I could do was wait until inspiration struck.

I put Kate in Christianne and Marie Claire's old bedroom, and as soon as I got her settled I went to find Fleur. I had some family business to attend to. She was in the kitchen. I sat down at the table and she poured me a cup of tea. I handed her the photo of Pierre standing in front of the barn with the sledge-hammer. She took one look at it and gasped.

"Where did you get this picture?" she demanded, clearly distraught.

"I met Pierre a few years ago. The circumstances aren't important. No, I didn't sleep with him. Anyway, he never told me who he was and I didn't recognize him. One night, he mysteriously disappeared again, but this time he left this pho-tograph under my door. As a child, I remember watching someone leave the house with a suitcase in the middle of the night. I thought it was a dream until this."

"Oh, Buddy," she said, suddenly very sad. She sat down next to me and hung her head low. "Remember how your birth interrupted Pierre's manhood ritual? After that, the other boys teased Pierre mercilessly, saying that he would never become a man.

"One night at supper, even Papa got into the act. Gaston was telling a story about catching Pierre wearing a dress and Papa said, 'Maybe Pierre sits down to pee.' We all laughed, Buddy, even Maman. So the next morning, when we got up and discovered him missing, we all felt guilty. But none so guilty as Papa. He wouldn't speak to anyone for days."

So that's why Papa was always so nice to me. He had felt guilty for driving one gay son out of the house and didn't want to do it to another. That must have been why he let me dance everywhere, and why he bought Davide that toy piano with a tiny candelabra on top. Fleur continued.

"For months we expected him to return, but he never did. Maman and Papa never spoke about it to us. Everyone felt bad and just wanted to forget about it. So we did. Until now."

"I'm sorry, Fleur," I said, sensing her pain. "Thank you for telling me the story. Good night." I kissed her, and then went up to my old room, mulling it all over in my head. I got in bed, but I couldn't sleep. For some reason I was aflame with desire. I wondered if Yves's porno stash was still under the bed. I reached down and sure enough found a stack of magazines. I opened up one of my old favorites, *Kept After School,* in which a sexy teacher spanks a bad boy and then fucks him on the desk. I went immediately to my favorite part, the page where she measures his cock with the ruler, and something fell out. It was the program for *Attiwapiskat.* I flipped through it. I had to admit, that show was years ahead of its time. But that was yesterday. I'd left the theater behind with all my illusions. Now I was just interested in getting off.

Later, as I was falling asleep with Cornygirl in my arms, I thought I heard someone singing far away. I lay there listening for a while. It was coming from the barn so I decided to investigate. I got dressed and quietly tiptoed barefoot down-stairs. Outside, the moon was a tiny sliver in the sky, yet it was bursting with the attitude of a full eclipse. God, how I loved that kind of confidence. I used to have that. Oh, well, best not to dwell on the past. Now I just had to find out who possessed that haunting voice. I went into the barn. It seemed as though the voice was coming from Persephone's pen. My God, a singing pig! I'd be rich. To get to the pen I had to walk across a lot of ancient pig manure, but I didn't care. After my time in L.A. a little bit of pig shit was just what I needed. Instead of a red carpet at an awards show in Hollywood, celebrities should be forced to negotiate a shitty field. That would keep them grounded.

When I reached the pen and looked in, I couldn't believe what I saw. My brother Guy was lying against Persephone, singing an old French folk song about broken dreams and missed opportunities, and even though it was a hundred years old and as hokey as a step dance, he made it seem somehow modern and urgent. Where had he been hiding his talent?

And what about me? What about my talent? I had been running from my true calling, theater, for far too long. It was time to get back up on the boards, but this time I would do it differently. I would not appear in the play. I knew that my voice, although world class, wasn't on par with Guy's. Besides, I would be far too busy writing, directing, and producing. No, it was clear. I had to make Guy the star. With that voice, the show was bound to be a huge hit, and we could pay off the mortgage. It was too much of a cliché not to work. I snuck back to the house and immediately phoned Marco to ask him for money.

"How's it going up there? Catch any moose?" he asked.

"No, just a lot of resentment and bitterness."

"It seems to follow you around."

"I'm calling because I need twenty thousand dollars."

"What's it for?"

"I'm putting on a show."

"Who do you play?"

"Actually, I've decided just to write and direct this time."

"That sounds like a very good idea."

"What are you trying to say?"

"Well, you haven't exactly set the acting world on fire. I'm talking to you as a friend here."

"It doesn't matter. I have my star. I discovered my brother

Guy has the most incredible voice. I'm so excited. I just saw him in the barn singing, lying against a pig."

"So the musical's about a pig?" he asked, not really listening. "Buddy, it sounds like a winner. Pork is making a real comeback, you know. I'm a vegetarian but even I can't refuse a piece of bacon."

"Marco, that's it! I'll do a show about pigs and pork. They say you should always write what you know. Songs about the history of pork, the importance of cooking it well, maybe even a number about famous pigs throughout history. Marco, you're a genius!"

"Good."

"I've got to go. I must start right away. Oh, I forgot. Can I have the money?"

"Of course, Buddy, I really like the idea of you not being in the show. Be sure to invite me to the premiere." It appeared that nobody believed in me. Let's face it, everything I had ever done had been a flop. I had failed as an actor, a model, a visual artist, and even as a husband and father. I vowed that this time, I would show them! No. I'd show myself! No. I'd show them.

A really big shew

The next few weeks were a whirlwind of activity. It had been a long time since I'd been in the center of a whirlwind. Well, my own whirlwind, that is, and it felt good. The first thing I had to do was convert the barn into a theater. Kate volunteered to stay and supervise the construction. Luckily, the copper mine had recently closed, resulting in a lot of unemployment in the area, so it was easy to scare up a crew. They were willing to work for nothing, which was good because it was all I could afford. In lieu of salaries, I had made everybody partners in the show.

Claude and Jean-Claude were the first to sign up. They were carpenters, and their shoddy workmanship was in evidence all over town. You could sure go a long way when you're good-looking twins. Even ugly twins do well. Look at the Olsen girls. Kate couldn't have been happier bossing a group of men around, and much to my surprise they all seemed to enjoy it, too. I could also see a real connection developing between her and Fleur. The day Fleur showed up with her head shaved, it was official—Kate was smitten. Kate loved bald girls.

St. Hubert sur la Lac had grown a lot since I had left. There was now a Gap, a Starbucks, and a Blockbuster Video. Madame Levesque's goiter, however, was still going strong. It had now officially passed the record set by *The Mousetrap*. Some things never change. People will always line up to see a freak. During a break from writing, I decided to finally catch the show. I'd dreamt about seeing it for years, and when I finally did it was such a letdown. Sort of like when I met Barbra Streisand and discovered that she was actually nice.

The first person I hired for the creative team was my brother Davide, to write and conduct the music. I found him in town, living alone in a cramped one-bedroom apartment where he gave private piano lessons. He looked much the same, and even though he was unmarried and had a shrine to Celine Dion, he still maintained that he was straight.

"Did you bring Tandy with you? She's really fetching."

"No, we divorced."

"Oh, that's too bad because she's really fetching, you know."

"So you said."

Then I went to see my sister Jeanne, who lived in a nice three-bedroom home with her husband, an unemployed miner, and their two kids. Oddly enough, she didn't seem so simple anymore, especially beside her husband, who was borderline retarded but absolutely gorgeous. In this neck of the woods they quite often went hand in hand. She made a living doing alterations and making dresses with Butterick patterns for the neighbours. Her specialty was wedding gowns. And even though she wasn't working at the moment, she made enough to support them. When I pitched her the idea for the show, she agreed on one condition—no wedding scenes. I told her my ideas and she started to sketch right away. It was really starting to happen. I wanted Guy for the lead but I knew he'd probably turn me down due to our acrimonious history. So one night, sitting alone with him at the table after dinner, I decided to make my move.

"What do you want from life, Guy?"

"It's too late to ask that."

"Okay. What did you want?"

"Nothing. I have everything I want right here."

"You have nothing here. Your best friends are a pig and a bottle. You could have so much more. You may not be the world's most beautiful man but you have a great chest. And I might be wrong, but I have a feeling that deep within that chest lurks a great voice."

"How do you know?" he asked defensively.

"Just guessing."

"Well, I can carry a tune," he admitted.

"Let's hear something. Don't be shy. I'm family."

"Well, okay." He paused, took in a deep breath, and began to sing a beautiful French folk song.

"There once was a girl named Marie,
Who blew seven bikers for free.
She swallowed it all and still wanted more,
So they gave her their hot stinking pee!"

"You have a beautiful voice. You've got to be in my show! And where do we get the rights to that song?"

"No way. I have big ears. Everyone will laugh at me."

"Guy, did you know that in Hollywood actors are paying thousands of dollars to get their ears enlarged? It's the hot new thing."

"But I'm no actor. I'd be so afraid in front of all those people."

"Would you feel better if I put Persephone in the show? After all, it's her farm, too."

"That would help. But still . . ."

"Guy, this show is going to save the farm. Everything depends upon you saying yes."

"Okay, I'll do it," he said. I knew he couldn't resist being the hero. Now that I had my star, I had to write the show. I got to work, and soon my spirits were soaring. Life began to make sense again. The first thing I did was name it: *Pork, the Musical.* Once you have a title, everything else falls into place. The rest was easy, and the easy was history.

Meanwhile, Kate and Fleur grew closer and closer. In fact, Fleur seemed reborn. Her beauty, which had been dimmed by age and bad times, began to reappear. I smelled love in the air. As for me, I couldn't stop thinking about Barclay Kent.

One night Kate, Fleur, Guy, and I were all sitting around the big table after a late dinner. I heard the sound of a plane coming in over the lake. My heart skipped a beat. I tried to play it cool.

"Maybe I'll just mosey on down to the dock and see who it is," I said casually. Kate would have none of it.

"It's your boyfriend Barclay," she said sarcastically.

"He's not my boyfriend. I just want to fuck him." Guy's ears went red.

"Jesus, do you have to spell it out for the world?" he sputtered.

"Oh, please, Belize." I grabbed two Irish coffees and ran to the dock. Barclay was in the midst of tying up his plane. He didn't see me so I watched him work. Well, stared at his ass. Finally he noticed me and looked up.

"What's your plane's name?" I asked him.

"Beechcraft."

"That's a brand name. What's it's name?"

"Plane?"

"No. A name, like Susan or Balthazar."

"It doesn't have a name, I guess."

"Oh, you have to give it a name, or terrible things will happen." I remembered the boy whose name I never knew and shuddered. "I name everything. I guess you could call it my philosophy. I even name every breath I take."

"What was that breath called?"

"Barclay." There was a silence.

"I just called that silence 'Buddy,' " he said.

"Oh, that's the nicest thing anyone has ever said to me. How could your wife have walked out on you?"

"I could say that it was her fault because she didn't listen to me. Or I could say it was my fault because I was away all the time. But the real reason is that she wasn't a man."

"Excuse me. I thought you just said your wife wasn't a man."

"She wasn't. She was a woman."

"So, are you implying that you're gay?"

"You mean you can't tell?" he asked.

"No, you seem so straight."

"Really? All my friends think I'm a real flamer." All of a sudden, I realized that he actually did read gay. I guess I just didn't want to see it. When I saw him flying a plane I just assumed he was incredibly butch. This was a horse of a different colour.

"We have a lot in common," I said. "We're both gay divorcees. Is there anyone now?"

"No, there was, but that's over. After my marriage broke up, I moved to New York. Started lifting weights, doing the whole circuit scene. I saw a lot of sunsets, fucked up, let me tell you. Did a lot of boys. Of course some of those boys were in their forties. I don't regret it though. I was making up for lost time. Then I met this guy, Rory, a real party boy. We started going together. It got real serious and then he started getting more and more into crystal and, well, you know the rest."

"What, you came home one night and found him in bed with a dog and a broomstick?"

"No, he stole my stereo. What about you? Are you seeing anyone?"

"Well, there might be someone. He's a bush pilot though. They're a solitary breed, I hear."

"Really. I hear they're the marrying kind."

"Is there a diamond involved?"

"Not so fast. Let's start with a kiss." He kissed me and desire coursed through me like electric eels. "Mama said knock me out." I pushed him down on the dock and straddled his chest.

"Look. You're going to get fucked and fucked good. You understand?" I could hardly believe that it was me talking.

"Pardon?"

"You heard me. Take your shirt off. Hurry! Now your pants. Come on. I don't have all day." Barclay did as he was told. Emboldened thus, I continued. "All right, your underwear. I want to see what you've got." He removed his briefs. I couldn't have been happier. Well, I could have. He turned around and showed me his ass.

"Take me, Buddy." So I did. Yes, dear reader, I, Buddy Cole, under a starry sky on a rickety dock in northern Quebec, topped someone for the very first time. (Yes, we were safe, dear reader. How dare you even ask?)

Now it was official. Granny Limp Dick was dead.

Opening night

Well, I'm here," cried out Marco, hopping off the pontoon of Barclay's seaplane and onto the dock. It was finally opening night, and he had flown in to attend.

"That goddamn Barclay almost killed us all."

"That's what makes it so much fun," Barclay said, hopping out gaily. He beamed when he saw me. I felt myself falling in love.

"Have you chosen a name yet?" I called out.

"I'm trying, but there's just too many to choose from. I bought *The Big Book of Baby Names*. How do you like "Courtney"? It's the number-one name for girls right now."

"Surely you can do better than that."

"I'll keep thinking."

"You think too much."

"I'm a thinker, Buddy."

"And I'm a man of action. Kiss me, flyboy." We kissed, and then I packed him off to pick up more guests.

I turned to Marco. "That's my new man, you know."

"Yes, Buddy, I know. He talked about you nonstop the whole trip. I couldn't hear a goddamned word. As long as you're happy, that's all that's important."

I showed Marco to his room. I put him in our parents' bedroom and could tell he wasn't impressed with his digs.

"So this is where they conceived all of you? Kudos to your father. I couldn't get an erection in a room like this. He must have been quite a man." He noticed a photo on the wall.

"Are these your parents?"

"No, that's Queen Elizabeth and Prince Phillip," I said.

"You look just like them." Marco opted to take a "quick restorative power nap" and I rushed over to the barn, which was now a beautiful theater. My cast had assembled onstage. They were a ragtag group of amateur actors, assembled from the top high school drama students, rejects from little theater, and the Alouette Quartet, a group of singing copper miners. They looked like racehorses eager to get out of the starting gate. I was so proud of them, especially Guy. He was extraordinary. But something was wrong. Then I noticed that Persephone was wearing the wrong costume—a horrible-looking big hat and a huge housedress.

"Persephone, that's not at all what we had agreed upon. You're supposed to be in the taffeta dress. And where are your shoes?"

"This is what she wanted to wear," said Guy, defending her.

"Guy, thank you for your concern, but with her dressed like that you might as well just cancel the show and burn down the barn."

"What difference does it make? She knows the choreography. She's brilliant in the part. Can't you cut her some slack?" I ignored him and turned back to the pig.

"You know what, Persephone? If you think that hat and blanket can hide your fat, you're sadly mistaken. You still look fat, just badly dressed and fat." Her eyes widened. I had never seen a pig so insulted in all my life. She thrust her snout in the air, turned, and walked off the stage in a huff. I had obviously touched a chord. She had been a complete professional throughout the whole rehearsal process, so this behaviour was completely out of character. I suppose all the attention had gone to her head. I had seen it happen before to lesser stars, Mackenzie Phillips for one.

"Fine!" I said to my stunned cast. "We'll do the show without her. Everyone into position."

"But Buddy, I—"

"Guy, please. I can only deal with one prima donna at a time."

"I'm no prima donna."

"Okay, that's it!" I exploded. "Rehearsal's canceled. Everyone be back here at five thirty for notes." I stormed out. I had to be alone, so I went to sit on the dock. Why was I putting myself through this torture? Then I thought about what I'd said to Persephone. Had I been too harsh? Pigs are supposed to be fat. A skinny pig is a sick pig.

While I was mulling this over, Barclay arrived with some surprise guests. Kurt Russell, Goldie Hawn, Martin Short and his wife, Nancy Dolman, all clambered out of the plane. Finally, celebrity cachet. My problems were solved. Even if Persephone never returned and the show stunk, we'd still make the front page. When Kurt got closer I realized that he had had his ears enlarged. Guy would be so happy. Then I rushed up to greet Goldie.

"Miss Hawn, it's a pleasure to meet you. I had a rabbit named after you." Goldie just clutched her purse a bit closer to her body. Then, looking at my watch, I realized I had to run back to the theater for final notes. It was a half hour to curtain and the house was filling up quickly. The box office manager told me that we were sold out. Could it be that I, Buddy Cole, finally had a hit on my hands?

I scanned the lobby for familiar faces. When my brother Yves came up to me, I almost didn't recognize him. He had gained at least sixty pounds and his facial features were sliding onto his shoulders. He had lost most of his hair and had really yellow teeth. His wife looked just like him. They lived about forty miles away, and had left their four kids at home to come see the play, Yves's first since *Attawapiskat*. They showed me their kids' photos, and I *ooohed* and *ahhed* at all the right moments, especially when I saw a picture of their oldest boy, Luc. It was obvious he wasn't just a nephew, he was a sister.

"This is my son who plays piano," said Yves. "I know he's like you. I don't care, but my wife can't handle it."

"I just don't think it's right," she said in a hundred-cigarette-a-day voice. Brother Aloysius also showed up. He must have been over eighty by now, but he looked much the same. He was beaming with pride.

"You've really gotten around, young man. I was really excited to hear that you married Tandy Porter. She's my favorite actress, you know. I don't watch TV, but I love to read the tabloids. This town really needs this show. It's been down in the dumps for too long, and all because of that infernal Blockbuster, but don't get me going. You know, Buddy, five years ago I could do anything. But it's different when you're eighty."

"Is there a big difference between seventy-five and eighty?"

"You'd be amazed. Well, I've got to go to the bathroom before the show starts. That's one of the differences. But I do what I can to keep young."

When he turned and walked away, I saw that he had a really curvy ass. I realized he was wearing Carma Norma Bum Pads for Men. What synchronicity. I felt like Carma had forgiven me and was smiling down on my production. After all, she'd financed it. The next thing I saw was unprecedented—Madame Levesque had arrived, surrounded by her entourage. She hadn't had a day off in thirty years. She came up to me.

"I wish you a lot of luck," she said. "This town is going to need a new show."

"Are you retiring, Madame Levesque?"

"Yes, I'm afraid so. I have cancer in my goiter."

"Oh, I'm sorry. Is there nothing they can do?"

"Well, they could cut it off, eh, but it would ruin my looks."

"I totally understand. Enjoy the show." Then there was a commotion at the door, so I went to investigate. A massively muscled Indian man with long black hair, about my age with two slutty looking blond girls on each arm, was arguing with one of the ushers. It was my old friend Merv.

"Let me in. The head guy's my friend," Merv yelled at the usher.

"But sir, you don't have tickets," he stammered.

"These people do not need tickets," I said, stepping in smoothly.

"Thanks, Buddy. I don't need any trouble, you know. You haven't changed a bit," he said, extending a powerful arm. I shook it. It was like sticking your hand in a vise. Nice.

"You certainly have. Did you join a gym?"

"Yeah. The Kingston Pen." He flexed. "Prison arms," he said.

"When did you get out?"

"A week ago. I've been partying ever since."

"Well, you deserve it. You're not a danger anymore. After all, you've only got one set of parents. You can't kill them twice. Who are your dates?"

"I don't know. I don't care. As long as they come across and keep their fingers out of my ass, I'm fine." They went in. I felt a tap on my shoulder.

"We're right back where we started from, aren't we, Buddy?" I recognized the voice instantly. It was Ronald Colman, looking as debonair as ever. Dianne stood by his side, still holding that damn rock. She had been holding on to that rock longer than Ann Miller had been holding on to her hairstyle.

"Oh, Ronald, it's so nice to see you," I said, hugging his British reserve tightly.

"You seem to have things under control," he said, gently prying me away.

"I'm coping. What brings you back to this neck of the woods, anyway?"

"Dianne and I live here. I manage the Blockbuster." I'd try not to seat them near Brother Aloysius.

"It's just so great to see you again," I said, hugging him again. "I want you to have the best stall in the house. We'll put you right up front where we used to kill the pigs. There's a lot of power there."

"We'll talk after the show," he said. "Dianne says hi." It was minutes before curtain and I had to get backstage. I saw Marco race in.

"Is it over?"

"No, it hasn't started."

He seemed disappointed. "Well, show me to my seat."

I took him to a box seat and rushed backstage. The curtain rose sharply at eight o'clock. The orchestra began the overture. Guy stepped out onstage and began to sing. It became apparent almost immediately that something was wrong. Every note was strangled and flat. His confidence seemed to leave him like air escaping a bag. Then it occurred to me. He couldn't sing without the pig by his side. Flop sweat formed on my brow. I had no choice but to find Persephone and bring her back. I found her in her dressing room, sour-faced and still in that awful outfit. She just stared into the mirror while I made my speech.

"Now, look. I know you're angry at me. That's fair. But look at the bigger picture. Who are you really hurting here? Me? Or Guy? You know damn well he can't sing without you. He's out there, trying to do a show to save this farm, and you're in here, wallowing in your own shit. You're going to throw all this away over a stupid hat? The only hat worth dying for is a crown. I know you don't like me, even though when we first met you licked my hand. Where was that trust that we once had? I realize that I hurt you, and I suppose an apology is in order. Now, I've never apologized to any human being in my life, but you're a pig, so I guess it's all right. I'm sorry." She continued to ignore me. It was up to the gods now.

I returned to the theater, where Act Two was in progress. It was the "Tribute to Great Pigs Through History" number. Guy was luckily not in it. There were tributes to Arnold Ziffle, Babe, Miss Piggy, Porky Pig, and Gordy. Guy's next number was the finale, so I would just have to wait and see. I stood in the wings, watching nervously. Kate came up to me.

"It's going fantastic! People love it! You've got a hit on your hands!"

"What are you talking about? Did you hear Guy in that opening number?"

"He was fine. People know it's an amateur production. Goldie's been laughing her shockingly well-preserved middle-aged ass off!"

"But I know he can be so much better. It's so frustrating." Then Guy came onstage for the finale. He opened his mouth to sing, but nothing came out. I could feel the audience tense up with anticipation. Then, from the back of the auditorium, I glimpsed a wet pink snout poke its way through the curtains. It was Persephone. She was wearing the "outfit." She looked like a queen. I was right, the outfit took a whole ham off her. She slowly began to walk down the aisle toward the stage. People in the audience turned and watched as she grandly made her way, every inch a star. Guy noticed her and let out a gasp. I signaled to Davide to begin the finale music once again. This time, Guy opened his mouth and the most won-drous sound came out. The audience was electrified.

Persephone made her way onstage. Guy beckoned her with open arms as she continued her inexorable porcine path toward him. Thank God the song was long, because that pig was slow. Persephone reached Guy just as he let loose the final note of the song. He embraced her, and the audience jumped to its feet, applauding and cheering. Not since Brent Carver won the Tony for *Kiss of the Spider Woman* had a Canadian audience been so thrilled. Then, from the stage-left balcony, a figure leaped onto the stage. He was carrying what looked like a cane or something. I figured it was just a crazed fan.

"Oh my God, it's Peter!" cried Kate. I looked closer and realized that it was indeed my brother Pierre and he was holding a sledgehammer. Before you could say "Don't," he brought it down hard on Persephone's head. She collapsed with an audible "oink." It was the first time I had ever actually heard her say it. I knew it was bad. Guy cried out in anguish and cradled the dying Persephone in his arms. Pierre threw down the hammer and looked at me, standing in the wings.

"Now I am a man!" he declared. And I thought *I* was the drama queen in the family. Then an amazing thing happened, something that the good people of St. Hubert sur la Lac still talk about to this day. From the box seats stage right, Dianne stood up and yelled.

"Here's your rock back, you little fucker!" She heaved her arm and threw the rock that she had been holding for so many years. It hit Pierre in the forehead, and he went down. I ran out onto the stage. Without thinking I knelt down beside Pierre. I could tell from the amount of blood pouring from his head that he was not long for this world.

"You ruined my show," I said in the sweetest voice I could muster.

"Got you back," he whispered and shrugged off this mortal coil. Would I ever do a show where a member of my family didn't die at the end? The next few minutes were a blur. Pierre was hauled off to the morgue, I was hauled off to the police station, and Persephone was hauled off to the butcher. After being questioned and telling them everything that I knew about Pierre, a.k.a. Peter, they let me go. Marco and Kate picked me up at the police station and took me home.

"Buddy," said Marco, "it was your best show ever. Despite the unfortunate carnage at the end, I listened to people as they filed out and everyone said they'd never had a better night at the theater. I just have one question. Why didn't you just take the twenty thousand dollars and pay off the farm's debt instead of spending all that money to mount a huge Broadway-style musical?"

"Marco, what kind of ending would that have been?"

When we got home Barclay was waiting for me on the dock. He had just got rid of Kurt and the gang. He took me in his arms and just held me for the longest time until my arms fell asleep. After waking them up we lay down on the dock and stared up at the stars.

"I'm sorry about your brother," he said tenderly.

"He had a hard life." There was a long silence.

"Why don't we call that silence Pierre?" said Barclay.

I began to sob. He held me until my tears stopped and my arms fell asleep again.

"Did you like the show?" I asked.

"I loved it." He loved it. "And I love you." This was the first time a man had ever actually said that to me. I decided to risk it.

"I love you, too," I replied. We kissed. He pulled away excitedly.

"I want to show you something," he said, jumping up.

"What is it?" I asked.

"It's a surprise." He got in his plane and taxied out, taking my heart with him. I couldn't believe that I had finally found love, and right in my own backyard. I watched him as he took off, gracefully ascending into the skies as coloured smoke poured out the tail end of the plane. He was skywriting. How butch. He started doing loops and circles in the air until he had spelled out *I LUV*. But as he came down on the first stroke of what I assumed was a U, the plane continued downward and crashed in a huge fireball into the middle of the lake. I knew we should have named that plane.

After the fact

Wit escapes me at the end of this long journey, and wisdom is nothing but wit plus time. So, while we wait for that time to come, let me update you, adored reader, on what has transpired since. Just snuggle up to me and enjoy your cigarette as I whisper the final words of *Buddy Babylon* in your ear.

Marco squandered his vast inheritance in less than a year. Luckily, he was in a minor car accident wherein he suffered whiplash and was awarded a huge settlement.

Kate and Fleur fell in love, and Kate moved into the farmhouse. The two of them now run the theater. *Pork, the Musical* is still running, and unemployment in the region has become a distant memory. Homosexuality, however, is on the rise.

Guy became a huge Canadian star and recently made his very first television appearance on a figure-skating special for the CBC. He got his ears fixed and is currently seeing a lovely young alcoholic actress from Stratford.

Ronald still runs the Blockbuster Video. Recently he and Brother Aloysius have become involved in a very vicious war of words in the letters section of the local paper. Dianne was found not guilty in her trial, and returned to driving. She started a taxicab company in St. Hubert sur la Lac, but made the mistake of hiring Claude and Jean-Claude as cabbies. Their work can be seen all over town.

Joey turned out to be HIV positive, but his health is better than ever. He swears it's the coke, but I think the protease inhibitors might have something to do with it. He recently competed in the International Mr. Leatherman Competition and was named Mr. Congeniality.

Ralph, however, was not so lucky. He passed away last year. He fell off the roof while trying to fix those damn shingles.

Grandma Schiratti sold the house and moved to Toronto. She now runs a bakery. She looks ten years younger, and has taken up Rollerblading. Will it never end?

Suzanne and Pleshette were cast in their own sitcom, *Good Girl, Bad Girl.* They play teenage policewomen. It recently passed *Chasin' Raisins* in the ratings, so in a desperate ploy, Tandy decided to come out as a lesbian on her show last season. It backfired and the show was canceled. I could have told her that. No one wants to see that on television.

I erected a memorial to Barclay on L'Isle des Memoires. It's a copper statue of him in his plane, shirtless. It's become a popular cruising spot for all the new homosexuals in town.

As for Henry, nothing's changed. Exactly the same as he always was. Isn't that right, Henry?

And as for me, I run a popular gay bar in Toronto now called Buddy's. My nephew Luc has come to work for me. He looks like Yves did, yet he acts like me. A real heartbreaker. Unclehood suits me. I guess you could say that I've finally found peace, although a letter just arrived from my old friend Kofi Annan, the Secretary General of the United Nations, asking me to intervene in a new catfight emerging in the Middle East. And you know, I just might.

Acknowledgments

The authors wish to acknowledge the following people who have helped in the development of Buddy Cole over the years, from his humble beginnings in Paul's basement in front of an ever present video camera, to his current incarnation as a published author: Carol Beauchamp for providing the spark that lit the flame; Diane Polley and Pam Thomas for discovering the *Kids in the Hall;* Lorne Michaels and Ivan Fecan for bringing the *Kids* to television; Cindy Park, Robert Boyd, Joe Forristal, Jeff Ross, Dan Redican, Betty Orr, and Jeff Berman for producing the damn show; our director John Blanchard for his ideas and guidance in the television monologues; Jeralyn Wraith, Judy Cooper Sealy, and Hillary Corbett for Buddy's look; *Kids* writers Brian Hartt, Norm Hiscock, Diane Flacks, and Frank van Keeken for their contributions; Al Miller and Bill Sims for being such road warriors; Rachel Sutherland for her love and guidance; Steven Surjik and Mark Sawyer for the Buddy films; the people at HBO, CBS, CBC, and Comedy Central for giving the *Kids* a cathode ray home; everyone at the Rivoli Club where Buddy first began to speak to his adoring public; Ralph Zimmerman for the early years and David Steinberg for the later; the *Kids in the Hall,* Dave Foley, Mark McKinney, Bruce McCulloch, and Kevin McDonald for their comic genius; Bruce LaBruce for *Super 8½;* Rob Rowatt for his video camera; Brian Hiltz for those wild Rivoli shows; Luciano Casimiri for Uncle Sappho; Doug Bergstrom and Guy Babineau for being hilarious; Sally Cochrane for hiring Scott at Second City; Tim Kazurinsky for providing the name; Terry Danuser for being the best manager ever; our literary agent Dean Willliamson for the harebrained idea of a Buddy book; our editor Tom Spain for his insight and tough love; his assistant Mitch Hoffman for his support and engaging telephone manner; Debra Theaker, Randall Finnerty, and Christine Bellini for their notes in the initial phases of the book; Tim Sims, Darlene Harrisson, and Karen Ballard (aka 'The Love Cats'); Barbara and Phillip Thompson, and Rena and Valdo Bellini for being our wonderful parents; Craig Thompson, Rand Thompson, Derek Thompson, and Dean Thompson for their brotherly love; and Stuart Bailey, Eric Casemiro, Warren Phillips, Gord Disley, Mike Thorner, and Tom King for their general creative support. For those people whom we may have forgotten, all blame lies at the feet of that ruthless monster called the deadline.

Paul Bellini began his career as a comedy writer with *The Kids in the Hall*, where he spent four seasons writing with Scott Thompson. His other credits include *Out There in Hollywood* (Comedy Central), *This Hour Has 22 Minutes* (CBC), and the independent film *Hayseed*.